How to W a JavaScript Chess Engine

FM Bill Jordan

FM Bill Jordan

Table of Contents

How to Write a JavaScript Chess Engine

6

Introduction

Other books on Chess programming include:

- The Joy of Chess Programming
- How to Write a Chess Program
- How to Write a BitBoard Chess Engine
- Advanced Chess Programming
- How to Write a Complex Chess Engine

I can easily make small changes and update this book. If you have any constructive suggestions you can email me at **swneerava@gmail.com**. Feel welcome to suggest topics for a Chess book you would like to see written. Positive reviews are welcome.

FM Bill Jordan

How to Write a JavaScript Chess Engine

It is assumed that you know the basic rules of Chess and Algebraic notation that is used to record Chess positions and moves.

The engine knows:

- The moves of the six types of pieces.
- Castling, including conditions which prevent castling.
- Pawn promotion.
- The *en passant capture*.
- Check and checkmate.
- Stalemate.
- Draw by triple repetition.
- Draw by the 50 move rule.
- etc.

Advantages to JavaScript

JavaScript is an *interpreted* language so you do not need a compiler to create an executable program. JavaScript source code can be edited with any text editor. I use the free RJ TextEd which is quite good. No doubt there are good alternatives. There is the option to use a dedicated JavaScript editor.

A JavaScript program can simply be run from a web browser. Popular browsers at the time of writing are Google Chrome, Mozilla Firefox, Safari, Microsoft Edge etc. To run a JavaScript Chess engine all you is a text editor and a web browser. The engine can be run offline or online.

The engine uses one html file and one JavaScript file.

- board.html
- engine2.js

The engine is an original program written by the author. You may download the above files from my Github page which is at **https://github.com/billjordanchess/JavaScript-Chess**. You can then run board.html which will launch the engine. If you run it offline you need to use the Safari browser. If you upload the files to a website it will in theory work with other browsers.

It will be helpful to know html and JavaScript.

Web Workers

It's possible to create a JavaScript Chess engine without a Web Worker, but it will run more smoothly with a web worker. A web worker can simply be added by adding some extra code.

There are some drawbacks. Running the engine offline is useful for debugging. One is a web worker cannot be used offline with all browsers. The only browser I know of that can be used offline with a Web Worker is Safari.

Normally, a large JavaScript program would be divided into several different modules. Most of the code is in one module so that only one web worker needs to be used.

Board and Piece Representation

Board Representation

There are various ways to represent a chessboard within a program. A simple method is to use an array of 64 elements. Each element represents one square of the chessboard. This engine uses this approach. Element 0 represents the A1 square in Algebraic notation, while element 63 represents the H8 square.

Piece Representation

Pieces are presented by the numbers 0-5 i.e.

- 0 = P = Pawn
- 1 = N = Knight
- 2 = B = Bishop
- 3 = R = Rook
- 4 = Q = Queen
- 5 = K = King
- 6 = EMPTY = Empty Square

```
const NORTH = 0;
const NE = 1;
const EAST = 2;
const SE = 3;
const SOUTH = 4;
const SW = 5;
const WEST = 6;
const NW = 7;
```

/* The 8 directions line pieces may move in, from White's end of the board. */

```
const P = 0;
const N = 1;
const B = 2;
```

```
const R = 3;
const Q = 4;
const K = 5;
```

/* The 6 types of pieces. */

```
const EMPTY = 6;
const MAX_PLY = 64; //Maximum search depth.
const MOVE_STACK = 2000;
const GAME_STACK = 2000;
const HASH_SCORE = 100000000;
const CAPTURE_SCORE = 10000000;
const A1 = 0, B1 = 1, C1 = 2, D1 = 3, E1 = 4, F1 = 5,
G1 = 6, H1 = 7;
const A2 = 8, B2 = 9, C2 = 10, D2 = 11, E2 = 12, F2 =
13, G2 = 14, H2 = 15;
const A3 = 16, B3 = 17, C3 = 18, D3 = 19, E3 = 20, F3
= 21, G3 = 22, H3 = 23;
const A4 = 24, B4 = 25, C4 = 26, D4 = 27, E4 = 28, F4
= 29, G4 = 30, H4 = 31;
const A5 = 32, B5 = 33, C5 = 34, D5 = 35, E5 = 36, F5
= 37, G5 = 38, H5 = 39;
const A6 = 40, B6 = 41, C6 = 42, D6 = 43, E6 = 44, F6
= 45, G6 = 6, H6 = 7;
const A7 = 48, B7 = 49, C7 = 50, D7 = 51, E7 = 52, F7
= 52, G7 = 54, H7 = 55;
const A8 = 56, B8 = 57, C8 = 58, D8 = 59, E8 = 60, F8
= 61, G8 = 62, H8 = 63;
```

/* The squares of the chessboard. Only some of these constants are used. However, any of them are potentially useful for debugging. */

```
var fen_name; //Used when loading or saving a position
as a FEN file.
var fixed_depth;
var max_time = 0;
var start_time = 0;
var stop_time;
var max_depth = 1;
var deep; //The deepest search reached.
var turn = 0;
var currentkey = 0;
var currentlock = 0;
var currentpawnkey = 0;
```

```
var currentpawnlock = 0;
var root_from, root_to, root_score; //The engine's
move.
var move_count; //Number of legal moves in a position.
var side = 0, xside = 1;
```

/* The side to move and the other side. xside was used as a
convention in eary engines such as GNUChess. */

```
var fifty = 0;
var ply = 0, hply = 0;
var nodes = 0;// The number of nodes (i.e. positions)
searched.
```

Create2DArray

r is the number of rows. **c1** is the number of columns.

```
function Create2DArray(r, c1) {
 var x = [];
 x.length = r;
 for (var i = 0; i < r; i++) {
  x[i] = [];
  x[i].length = c1;
  for (var j = 0; j < c1; j++) {
   x[i][j] = 0;
  }
 }
 return x;
}
```

Single dimensional arrays are easy to create in JavaScript. For
example, **var x = []; x.length = r;** creates an array called x with a
length of r. However, multi dimensional arrays are more complex.
Create2DArray() is used to create them using a loop.

Create3DArray

r is the length of the first dimension. **c1** is the length of the second
dimension. **c2** is the length of the third dimension.

```
function Create3DArray(r, c1, c2) {
 var x = [];
```

```
 x.length = r;
 for (var i = 0; i < r; i++) {
  x[i] = [];
  x[i].length = c1;
  for (var j = 0; j < c1; j++) {
   x[i][j] = [];
   x[i][j].length = c2;
   for (var k = 0; k < c1; k++) {
    x[i][j][k] = 0;
   }
  }
 }
 return x;
}
```

Create3DArray() is used to create a 3-dimensional array.

Algebraic

sq is a square.

```
function Algebraic(x) {
 const file = 'abcdefgh'[COL[sq]];
 const rank = ROW[sq] + 1;
 return file + rank;
}
```

Algebraic() converts a square number from 0-63 to Algebraic notation. For example, if x was 63 it would return **h8**. This is used to display moves.

LongAlgebraic

p is the moving piece. **from** is the from square. **to** is the to square. **capture** is the capture value.

```
function LongAlgebraic(p, from, to, capture) {
 var piece = piece_char[p];
 if (p == P) piece = "";
 const file = 'abcdefgh'[COL[from]];
 const rank = ROW[from] + 1;
 var hyphen = "-";
 if (capture != EMPTY) hyphen = "x";
```

```
    return piece + file + rank + hyphen + Algebraic(to);
}
```

LongAlgebraic() returns a string containing the initial letter of the moving piece (unless it is pawn) and the **from** and **to** squares in Algebraic, separated by a hyphen. If the move is a capture an 'X' is used instead of a hyphen.

Move

```
function Move() {
  var from = 0;
  var to = 0;
  var promote = 0;
  var score = 0;
}
```

Move() stores data for a single move in conjunction with **move_list**. **from** and **to** are used to store the move. **promote** is only used if the move is a pawn promotion. **score** is used to sort moves. Moves with higher scores are searched first.

Game

```
function Game() {
  var from = 0;
  var to = 0;
  var promote = 0;
  var capture = 0;
  var fifty = 0;
  var castle_q0 = 0;
  var castle_q1 = 0;
  var castle_k0 = 0;
  var castle_k1 = 0;
  var start_piece = 0;
}
```

Game() stores data for a single move in conjunction with **game_list**.

- **from, to** and **promote** are similar to the same variables in **Move()**.

- **capture** stores the type of piece captured, if any. This is used when the move is taken back.
- **fifty** stores the number of half-moves since the last pawn move or capture.
- The 4 castle variables store which types of castling are possible.
- **start_piece** is used to undo promotion.

```javascript
var move_list = [];
var game_list = [];
var Kingloc = []; Kingloc.length = 2;
var Table_score = []; Table_score.length = 2;
var Pawn_mat = []; Pawn_mat.length = 2;
var Piece_mat = []; Piece_mat.length = 2;
var board = []; board.length = 64;
var color = []; color.length = 64;
var first_move = []; first_move.length = 64;
var mask = []; mask.length = 64;
var not_mask = []; not_mask.length = 64;
var Hist = new Create2DArray(64, 64);
var square_score = new Create3DArray(2, 7, 64);
var LineMoves = new Create2DArray(64, 9);
var KnightMoves = new Create2DArray(64, 9);
var KingMoves = new Create2DArray(64, 9);
var bit_pieces = new Create2DArray(2, 7);
var King_endgame = new Create2DArray(2, 64);
var Passed = new Create2DArray(2, 64);
var mask_passed = new Create2DArray(2, 64);
var mask_isolated = new Create2DArray(2, 64);
var PawnMove = new Create2DArray(2, 64);
var PawnDouble = new Create2DArray(2, 64);
var pawncaptures = new Create2DArray(2, 64);
var PawnCaptureLeft = new Create2DArray(2, 64);
var PawnCaptureRight = new Create2DArray(2, 64);
var rank = new Create2DArray(2, 64);

const ISOLATED_SCORE = [-20, 20];// Used for isolated
pawns.
const piece_char = ["P", 'N', 'B', 'R', 'Q', 'K'];
const piece_value = [100, 300, 300, 500, 900, 10000];
```

Board Arrays

```
const INIT_COLOR = [
  0, 0, 0, 0, 0, 0, 0, 0,
  0, 0, 0, 0, 0, 0, 0, 0,
  6, 6, 6, 6, 6, 6, 6, 6,
  6, 6, 6, 6, 6, 6, 6, 6,
  6, 6, 6, 6, 6, 6, 6, 6,
  6, 6, 6, 6, 6, 6, 6, 6,
  1, 1, 1, 1, 1, 1, 1, 1,
  1, 1, 1, 1, 1, 1, 1, 1
];
```

INIT_COLOR[] stores the starting position. These tables are copied to **board[]** and **color[]** when a game starts.

```
const INIT_PIECE = [
  3, 1, 2, 4, 5, 2, 1, 3,
  0, 0, 0, 0, 0, 0, 0, 0,
  6, 6, 6, 6, 6, 6, 6, 6,
  6, 6, 6, 6, 6, 6, 6, 6,
  6, 6, 6, 6, 6, 6, 6, 6,
  6, 6, 6, 6, 6, 6, 6, 6,
  0, 0, 0, 0, 0, 0, 0, 0,
  3, 1, 2, 4, 5, 2, 1, 3
];
```

INIT_PIECE[] stores the starting position. These tables are copied to **board[]** and **color[]** when a game starts.

```
const FLIP_BOARD = [
  56, 57, 58, 59, 60, 61, 62, 63,
  48, 49, 50, 51, 52, 53, 54, 55,
  40, 41, 42, 43, 44, 45, 46, 47,
  32, 33, 34, 35, 36, 37, 38, 39,
  24, 25, 26, 27, 28, 29, 30, 31,
  16, 17, 18, 19, 20, 21, 22, 23,
  8, 9, 10, 11, 12, 13, 14, 15,
  0, 1, 2, 3, 4, 5, 6, 7
];
```

FLIP_BOARD[] fetches the reverse number of a square. This is useful when populating [2][64] arrays in which the importance of squares may be very different for White and Black. For example, a white pawn on A2 has a very different value than a Black pawn on A2.

```
const COL = [
  0, 1, 2, 3, 4, 5, 6, 7,
  0, 1, 2, 3, 4, 5, 6, 7,
  0, 1, 2, 3, 4, 5, 6, 7,
  0, 1, 2, 3, 4, 5, 6, 7,
  0, 1, 2, 3, 4, 5, 6, 7,
  0, 1, 2, 3, 4, 5, 6, 7,
  0, 1, 2, 3, 4, 5, 6, 7,
  0, 1, 2, 3, 4, 5, 6, 7
];
```

COL[] can be used to look up the file(0-7) a given square is on. For example, COL[E1] would return 4.

```
const ROW = [
  0, 0, 0, 0, 0, 0, 0, 0,
  1, 1, 1, 1, 1, 1, 1, 1,
  2, 2, 2, 2, 2, 2, 2, 2,
  3, 3, 3, 3, 3, 3, 3, 3,
  4, 4, 4, 4, 4, 4, 4, 4,
  5, 5, 5, 5, 5, 5, 5, 5,
  6, 6, 6, 6, 6, 6, 6, 6,
  7, 7, 7, 7, 7, 7, 7, 7
];
```

ROW[] can be used to look up the rank(0-7) a given square is on. For example, ROW[E6] would return 5.

```
const NW_DIAG = [
  14, 13, 12, 11, 10, 9, 8, 7,
  13, 12, 11, 10, 9, 8, 7, 6,
  12, 11, 10, 9, 8, 7, 6, 5,
  11, 10, 9, 8, 7, 6, 5, 4,
  10, 9, 8, 7, 6, 5, 4, 3,
  9, 8, 7, 6, 5, 4, 3, 2,
  8, 7, 6, 5, 4, 3, 2, 1,
  7, 6, 5, 4, 3, 2, 1, 0
];
```

Every square on the board is intersected by 2 diagonals, except for the corner squares. The names NW and NE, are arbitrary, based on what the diagonals look like in the code.

NW_DIAG[] can be used to look up the nw diagonal(0-14) a given square is on. For example, NW_DIAG[B1] would return 13.

```
const NE_DIAG = [
  7, 8, 9, 10, 11, 12, 13, 14,
  6, 7, 8, 9, 10, 11, 12, 13,
  5, 6, 7, 8, 9, 10, 11, 12,
  4, 5, 6, 7, 8, 9, 10, 11,
  3, 4, 5, 6, 7, 8, 9, 10,
  2, 3, 4, 5, 6, 7, 8, 9,
  1, 2, 3, 4, 5, 6, 7, 8,
  0, 1, 2, 3, 4, 5, 6, 7
];
```

NE_DIAG[] can be used to look up the ne diagonal(0-14) a given square is on. For example, NE_DIAG[B1] would return 8.

PAWN_SCORE

```
const PAWN_SCORE = [
  0, 0, 0, 0, 0, 0, 0, 0,
  0, 2, 4, -12, -12, 4, 2, 0,
  0, 2, 4, 4, 4, 4, 2, 0,
  0, 2, 4, 8, 8, 4, 2, 0,
  0, 2, 4, 8, 8, 4, 2, 0,
  4, 8, 10, 16, 16, 10, 8, 4,
  100, 100, 100, 100, 100, 100, 100, 100,
  0, 0, 0, 0, 0, 0, 0, 0
];
```

PAWN_SCORE[] returns a score for a pawn on a given square.

- There is a penalty for unmoved d-pawns and e-pawns.
- There is a small bonus for pawns on more central files.
- There is a bonus for pawns in the centre.
- There is a bonus for pawns on the 6th rank.
- There is a large bonus for pawns on the 7th rank.

KNIGHT_SCORE

```
const KNIGHT_SCORE = [
 -30, -20, -10, -8, -8, -10, -20, -30,
 -16, -6, -2, 0, 0, -2, -6, -16,
 -8, -2, 4, 6, 6, 4, -2, -8,
 -5, 0, 6, 8, 8, 6, 0, -5,
 -5, 0, 6, 8, 8, 6, 0, -5,
 -10, -2, 4, 6, 6, 4, -2, -10,
 -20, -10, -2, 0, 0, -2, -10, -20,
 -150, -20, -10, -5, -5, -10, -20, -150
];
```

KNIGHT_SCORE[] returns a score for a knight on a given square. The closer the knight is to the centre, the better the score. Knights are weak on the edges. Knights are weak in the corners, especially on the opponent's side of the board.

BISHOP_SCORE

```
const BISHOP_SCORE = [
 -10, -10, -12, -10, -10, -12, -10, -10,
 0, 4, 4, 4, 4, 4, 4, 0,
 2, 4, 6, 6, 6, 6, 4, 2,
 2, 4, 6, 8, 8, 6, 4, 2,
 2, 4, 6, 8, 8, 6, 4, 2,
 2, 4, 6, 6, 6, 6, 4, 2,
 -10, 4, 4, 4, 4, 4, 4, -10,
 -10, -10, -10, -10, -10, -10, -10, -10
];
```

BISHOP_SCORE[] returns a score for a bishop on a given square. The closer the bishop is to the centre, the better the score.

ROOK_SCORE

```
const ROOK_SCORE = [
 4, 4, 4, 6, 6, 4, 4, 4,
 0, 0, 0, 0, 0, 0, 0, 0,
 0, 0, 0, 0, 0, 0, 0, 0,
 0, 0, 0, 0, 0, 0, 0, 0,
 0, 0, 0, 0, 0, 0, 0, 0,
 0, 0, 0, 0, 0, 0, 0, 0,
 20, 20, 20, 20, 20, 20, 20, 20,
```

```
 10, 10, 10, 10, 10, 10, 10, 10
];
```

ROOK_SCORE[] returns a score for a rook on a given square. On an empty board, a Rook may move to 14 squares, from any square. However, the Rook is often blocked by pawns of the same side.

The Rook scores more on the 1st, 7th and 8th ranks. It cannot be blocked by pawns of either side on the 1st or 8th ranks, while on the 7th rank it cannot be blocked by an opponent pawn defended by a pawn. There is a small bonus for being on the 1st rank and on a central file.

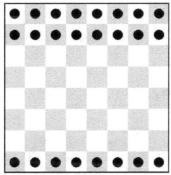

A white rook would get a bonus on any of the highlighted squares.

QUEEN_SCORE

```
const QUEEN_SCORE = [
 -10, -10, -6, -4, -4, -6, -10, -10,
 -10, 2, 2, 2, 2, 2, 2, -10,
 2, 2, 2, 3, 3, 2, 2, 2,
 2, 2, 3, 4, 4, 3, 2, 2,
 2, 2, 3, 4, 4, 3, 2, 2,
 2, 2, 2, 3, 3, 2, 2, 2,
 -10, 2, 2, 2, 2, 2, 2, -10,
 -10, -10, 2, 2, 2, 2, -10, -10
];
```

QUEEN_SCORE[] returns a score for a queen on a given square. The closer the queen is to the centre, the better the score.

21

King Tables

Two tables are used for the king. While the value of the square a piece is on does not change much for other pieces, it changes drastically for kings when an endgame is reached. A rather crude method is used to determine whether or not it is an endgame.

If the opponent has a queen, it is determined to be a middlegame and the first table is used.

The second table is used if the opponent does not have a queen.

Note that if one player has a queen and their opponent does not, the side with the queen can usually move their king into the centre with impunity.

KING_SCORE

```
const KING_SCORE = [
 20,  20,  20, -40,  10, -60,  20,  20,
 15,  20, -25, -30, -30, -45,  20,  15,
-48, -48, -48, -48, -48, -48, -48, -48,
-48, -48, -48, -48, -48, -48, -48, -48,
-48, -48, -48, -48, -48, -48, -48, -48,
-48, -48, -48, -48, -48, -48, -48, -48,
-48, -48, -48, -48, -48, -48, -48, -48,
-50, -50, -50, -50, -50, -50, -50, -50
];
```

KING_SCORE[] returns a score for a king on a given square when the opponent has a queen. The king is best on the first or second ranks and in or near the corner.

KING_ENDGAME_SCORE

```
const KING_ENDGAME_SCORE = [
 0,  8, 16, 18, 18, 16,  8,  0,
 8, 16, 24, 32, 32, 24, 16,  8,
16, 24, 32, 40, 40, 32, 24, 16,
25, 32, 40, 48, 48, 40, 32, 25,
25, 32, 40, 48, 48, 40, 32, 25,
16, 24, 32, 40, 40, 32, 24, 16,
```

```
8,  16, 24, 32, 32, 24, 16,  8,
0,  8, 16, 18, 18, 16,  8,  0
];
```

KING_ENDGAME_SCORE[] returns a score for a king on a given square when the opponent **does not** have a queen. The closer the king is to the centre, the better the score.

PASSED_SCORE

```
const PASSED_SCORE = [
 0,  0,  0,  0,  0,  0,  0,  0,
 0,  0,  0,  0,  0,  0,  0,  0,
60, 60, 60, 60, 60, 60, 60, 60,
30, 30, 30, 30, 30, 30, 30, 30,
15, 15, 15, 15, 15, 15, 15, 15,
 8,  8,  8,  8,  8,  8,  8,  8,
 8,  8,  8,  8,  8,  8,  8,  8,
 0,  0,  0,  0,  0,  0,  0,  0
];
```

PASSED_SCORE[] returns a bonus score if a pawn on the given square is passed. Note that a pawn on the seventh rank is always passed and has a bonus score of 100 as per the pawn_score table.

board

```
var board = [
 3, 1, 2, 4, 5, 2, 1, 3,
 0, 0, 0, 0, 0, 0, 0, 0,
 6, 6, 6, 6, 6, 6, 6, 6,
 6, 6, 6, 6, 6, 6, 6, 6,
 6, 6, 6, 6, 6, 6, 6, 6,
 6, 6, 6, 6, 6, 6, 6, 6,
 0, 0, 0, 0, 0, 0, 0, 0,
 3, 1, 2, 4, 5, 2, 1, 3
];
```

board[] represents the board. It is initialised with the starting position of the pieces. 0 = pawn, 1 = knight, 2 = bishop, 3 = rook, 4 = queen, 5 = king, 6 = empty.

color

```
var color = [
  0, 0, 0, 0, 0, 0, 0, 0,
  0, 0, 0, 0, 0, 0, 0, 0,
  6, 6, 6, 6, 6, 6, 6, 6,
  6, 6, 6, 6, 6, 6, 6, 6,
  6, 6, 6, 6, 6, 6, 6, 6,
  6, 6, 6, 6, 6, 6, 6, 6,
  1, 1, 1, 1, 1, 1, 1, 1,
  1, 1, 1, 1, 1, 1, 1, 1
];
```

color[] represents square colours. It is initialised with the starting colours of each square. 0 = white, 1 = black, 6 = empty.

```
var c = CAPTURE_SCORE;
const PawnCapScore = [0 + c, c + 100, c + 200, c +
300, c + 400];
const KnightCapScore = [c - 30, c + 70, c + 170, c +
270, c + 370];
const BishopCapScore = [c - 30, c + 70, c + 170, c +
270, c + 370];
const RookCapScore = [c - 50, c + 50, c + 150, c +
250, c + 350];
const QueenCapScore = [c - 90, c + 10, c + 110, c +
210, c + 310];
const KingCapScore = [c + 0, c + 100, c + 200, c +
300, c + 400];
```

Capture Score

The above arrays contain the scores of different types of captures. For example, PawnCapScore refers to captures by a pawn, in the order Pawn, Knight, Bishop, Rook and Queen.

It uses the MVLA formula (Most Valuable captured piece, least valuable Attacker). Scores are calculated by multiplying the ranking of the captured piece X 100, substracting the ranking of the capturing piece X 10, and adding the result to CAPTURE_SCORE.

P X Q scores high (c + 400), because the attacker gains material even if the Queen is defended. Q X P scores low (c - 90), because the attacker loses material if the pawn is defended.

Using these Lookup tables is much faster than calculating these scores on the fly.

Functions

SetUp

```
function SetUp() {
 SetTables();
 RandomizeHashTables();
 SetHashTables();
 SetPawns();
 SetMoves();
 SetBits();
 SetPassed();
 InitBoard();
}
```

SetUp() calls several functions when the program first begins. These are not called again, even if multiple games are played. **InitBoard()** is an exception. It is called each time a new game starts.

SetTables

```
function SetTables() {
 for (var x = 0; x < MOVE_STACK; x++) {
  move_list.push(new Move());
  game_list.push(new Game());
 }
 for (x = 0; x < 64; x++) {
  first_move[x] = 0;
 }
 for (x = 0; x < 64; x++) {
  square_score[0][P][x] = PAWN_SCORE[x] + 100;
  square_score[0][N][x] = KNIGHT_SCORE[x] + 300;
  square_score[0][B][x] = BISHOP_SCORE[x] + 300;
  square_score[0][R][x] = ROOK_SCORE[x] + 500;
  square_score[0][Q][x] = QUEEN_SCORE[x] + 900;
  square_score[0][K][x] = KING_SCORE[x];
  square_score[0][6][x] = 0;
 }
 var f;
 for (x = 0; x < 64; x++) {
  f = FLIP_BOARD[x];
```

```
  square_score[1][P][x] = PAWN_SCORE[f] + 100;
  square_score[1][N][x] = KNIGHT_SCORE[f] + 300;
  square_score[1][B][x] = BISHOP_SCORE[f] + 300;
  square_score[1][R][x] = ROOK_SCORE[f] + 500;
  square_score[1][Q][x] = QUEEN_SCORE[f] + 900;
  square_score[1][K][x] = KING_SCORE[f];
  square_score[1][6][x] = 0;
  King_endgame[0][x] = KING_ENDGAME_SCORE[x] -
square_score[0][5][x];
  King_endgame[1][x] = KING_ENDGAME_SCORE[x] -
square_score[1][5][x];
  Passed[0][x] = PASSED_SCORE[f];
  Passed[1][x] = -PASSED_SCORE[x];
 }
}
```

SetTables() creates the history tables. The multi-dimensial arrays **move_list[]** and **game_list[]** are populated.

The square score tables, the king endgame tables and the passed pawn tables are populated.

The hash tables are filled with random numbers.

SetPawns

```
function SetPawns() {
 for (x = A1; x <= H7; x++) {
  PawnMove[0][x] = x + 8;
 }
 for (x = A2; x <= H8; x++) {
  PawnMove[1][x] = x - 8;
 }
 for (x = A2; x <= H2; x++) {
  PawnDouble[0][x] = x + 16;
 }
 for (x = A7; x <= H7; x++) {
  PawnDouble[1][x] = x - 16;
 }
 for (x = A2; x <= H7; x++) {
  if (COL[x] > 0) {
   PawnCaptureLeft[0][x] = x + 7;
   PawnCaptureLeft[1][x] = x - 9;
  }
  else {
```

```
    PawnCaptureLeft[0][x] = x;
    PawnCaptureLeft[1][x] = x;
   }
   if (COL[x] < 7) {
    PawnCaptureRight[0][x] = x + 9;
    PawnCaptureRight[1][x] = x - 7;
   }
   else {
    PawnCaptureRight[0][x] = x;
    PawnCaptureRight[1][x] = x;
   }
  }
  for (var x = 0; x < 64; x++) {
   rank[0][x] = ROW[x];
   rank[1][x] = 7 - ROW[x];
  }
 }
```

SetPawns() populates the look-up tables **PawnMoves**, **PawnDouble**, **PawnCaptureLeft** and **PawnCaptureRight**. These are used when generating pawn moves, captures and attacks. This makes the code faster and easier to read. White pawns on the a-file cannot capture left, while on the h-file cannot capture right. If a white pawn on the a-file attempts to capture left, it will refer to the square the white pawn is on.

SetMoves

```
function SetMoves() {
 var k = 0;
 var x, y, z;
 for (x = 0; x < 64; x++) {
  k = 0;
  if (ROW[x] < 6 && COL[x] < 7)
   KnightMoves[x][k++] = x + 17;
  if (ROW[x] < 7 && COL[x] < 6)
   KnightMoves[x][k++] = x + 10;
  if (ROW[x] < 6 && COL[x] > 0)
   KnightMoves[x][k++] = x + 15;
  if (ROW[x] < 7 && COL[x] > 1)
   KnightMoves[x][k++] = x + 6;
  if (ROW[x] > 1 && COL[x] < 7)
   KnightMoves[x][k++] = x - 15;
  if (ROW[x] > 0 && COL[x] < 6)
   KnightMoves[x][k++] = x - 6;
```

```
  if (ROW[x] > 1 && COL[x] > 0)
   KnightMoves[x][k++] = x - 17;
  if (ROW[x] > 0 && COL[x] > 1)
   KnightMoves[x][k++] = x - 10;
  KnightMoves[x][k] = -1;
 }
 for (x = 0; x < 64; x++) {
  k = 0;
  for (z = 0; z < 8; z++)
   LineMoves[x][z] = -1;
  if (COL[x] > 0) LineMoves[x][WEST] = x - 1;
  if (COL[x] < 7) LineMoves[x][EAST] = x + 1;
  if (ROW[x] > 0) LineMoves[x][SOUTH] = x - 8;
  if (ROW[x] < 7) LineMoves[x][NORTH] = x + 8;
  if (COL[x] < 7 && ROW[x] < 7) LineMoves[x][NE] = x +
9;
  if (COL[x] > 0 && ROW[x] < 7) LineMoves[x][NW] = x +
7;
  if (COL[x] > 0 && ROW[x] > 0) LineMoves[x][SW] = x -
9;
  if (COL[x] < 7 && ROW[x] > 0) LineMoves[x][SE] = x -
7;
  y = 0;
  if (COL[x] > 0)
   KingMoves[x][y++] = x - 1;
  if (COL[x] < 7)
   KingMoves[x][y++] = x + 1;
  if (ROW[x] > 0)
   KingMoves[x][y++] = x - 8;
  if (ROW[x] < 7)
   KingMoves[x][y++] = x + 8;
  if (COL[x] < 7 && ROW[x] < 7)
   KingMoves[x][y++] = x + 9;
  if (COL[x] > 0 && ROW[x] < 7)
   KingMoves[x][y++] = x + 7;
  if (COL[x] > 0 && ROW[x] > 0)
   KingMoves[x][y++] = x - 9;
  if (COL[x] < 7 && ROW[x] > 0)
   KingMoves[x][y++] = x - 7;
  KingMoves[x][y] = -1;
 }
}
```

SetMoves() is called once at the start of a program to create *lookup tables* for moves of all units, except the pawns. This makes the move generation code simpler and much faster.

KnightMoves[][] stores all the knight moves possible from each square.

KingMoves[][] does the same for the king.

LineMoves[][] does the same for rooks, bishops and queens. **If** statements are used to prevent moves off the edge of the board being generated.

SetBits

```
function SetBits() {
 var x, y;
 for (x = 0; x < 2; x++) {
  for (y = 0; y < 7; y++)
   bit_pieces[x][y] = 0;
 }
 for (x = 0; x < 64; x++)
  mask[x] = (1 << x);
 for (x = 0; x < 64; x++)
  not_mask[x] = ~mask[x];
 for (x = 0; x < 64; x++) {
  mask_isolated[x] = 0;
  for (y = 0; y < 64; y++) {
   if (Math.abs(COL[x] - COL[y]) == 1)
    mask_isolated[x] |= (1 << y);
  }
 }
}
```

SetBits() initialises the values for various bitboards. **mask** represents the bitboard of a single square. **not_mask** represents all the square not in the bitboard. **mask_isolated[]** is used to tell if a pawn is isolated. Only a few bitwise operations are used in this program to keep it simple.

SetPassed

```
function SetPassed() {
 for (var x = 0; x < 64; x++) {
  mask_passed[0][x] = 0;
  mask_passed[1][x] = 0;
  for (var y = 0; y < 64; y++) {
```

```
  if (Math.abs(COL[x] - COL[y]) < 2) {
   if (ROW[x] < ROW[y] && ROW[y] < 7)
    mask_passed[0][x] |= (1 << y);
   if (ROW[x] > ROW[y] && ROW[y] > 0)
    mask_passed[1][x] |= (1 << y);
  }
 }
 }
}
```

SetPassed() initialises the values of **mask_passed[]**.
mask_passed[] is used to tell if a pawn is passed. If the opponent
has any pawns in the mask_passed of a pawn, then the pawn is not
passed.

InitBoard

```
function InitBoard() {
 var i;
 for (i = 0; i < 64; i++) {
  color[i] = INIT_COLOR[i];
  board[i] = INIT_PIECE[i];
 }
 side = 0;
 xside = 1;
 fifty = 0;
 ply = 0;
 hply = 0;
 first_move[0] = 0;
 Kingloc[0] = E1;
 Kingloc[1] = E8;
 SetCastle(1);
}
```

InitBoard() gets ready for a new game.

SetCastle

flag is true or false (0 or 1).

```
function SetCastle(flag) {
 game_list[0].castle_q0 = flag;
 game_list[0].castle_q1 = flag;
 game_list[0].castle_k0 = flag;
```

```
  game_list[0].castle_k1 = flag;
}
```

SetCastle() sets castling queenside and kingside permissions for both sides. 0 means a player cannot castle on that side while 1 means they can.

NewPosition

```
function NewPosition() {
 var i;
 var s;
 Piece_mat[0] = Pawn_mat[0] = Table_score[0] = 0;
 Piece_mat[1] = Pawn_mat[1] = Table_score[1] = 0;
 for (i = 0; i < 64; i++) {
  if (board[i] != EMPTY) {
    s = color[i];
    AddPiece(s, board[i], i);
   }
 }
 currentkey = GetKey();
 currentlock = GetLock();
}
```

NewPosition() sets up a new position. This is either from the start position or a position loaded from a FEN file.

Move Generation

```
function Gen() {
 move_count = first_move[ply];
 if (hply > 0)
  GenEp();
 GenCastle();
 for (var x = 0; x < 64; x++) {
  if (color[x] == side) {
   switch (board[x]) {
    case P:
     GenPawn(x);
     break;
    case N:
     GenKnight(x);
     break;
    case B:
     GenBishop(x, NE);
     GenBishop(x, SE);
     GenBishop(x, SW);
     GenBishop(x, NW);
     break;
    case R:
     GenRook(x, NORTH);
     GenRook(x, EAST);
     GenRook(x, SOUTH);
     GenRook(x, WEST);
     break;
    case Q:
     GenQueen(x, NE);
     GenQueen(x, SE);
     GenQueen(x, SW);
     GenQueen(x, NW);
     GenQueen(x, NORTH);
     GenQueen(x, EAST);
     GenQueen(x, SOUTH);
     GenQueen(x, WEST);
     break;
    case K:
     GenKing(x);
     break;
    default:
     break;
   }
```

```
    }
  }
  first_move[ply + 1] = move_count;
}
```

Gen

Gen() generates all moves for one side.

- It checks if an *en passant* capture is possible.
- It checks if castling is possible.
- It loops through the board searching for pieces of the side to move.
- Different functions are called for each type of piece.
- Bishops, rooks and queens call a function for each direction that they can move in.

GenEp

```
function GenEp() {
 var ep = game_list[hply - 1].to;
 if (board[ep] == 0 && color[ep] == xside &&
Math.abs(game_list[hply - 1].from - ep) == 16) {
  if (COL[ep] > 0 && color[ep - 1] == side && board[ep
- 1] == P) {
    AddCapture(ep - 1, PawnMove[side][ep], 10);
  }
  if (COL[ep] < 7 && color[ep + 1] == side && board[ep
+ 1] == P) {
    AddCapture(ep + 1, PawnMove[side][ep], 10);
  }
 }
}
```

GenEp() sees if an *en passant* capture is possible. It looks at the last move played. If it was a pawn move and the absolute difference between the from and to squares is 16, then it was a double pawn move. If so, it sees if there is an opponent pawn next to it. If there is, it adds the *en passant* capture to the move list.

Note that sometimes two *en passant* captures may be possible.

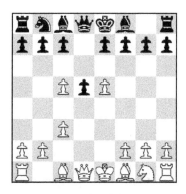

Black has just played **d7-d5**. Both **exd6** and **cxd6** are possible.

GenCastle

```
function GenCastle() {
 if (side == 0) {
  if (game_list[hply].castle_k0 > 0) {
   if (board[F1] == EMPTY && board[G1] == EMPTY) {
    AddMove(E1, G1);
   }
  }
  if (game_list[hply].castle_q0 > 0) {
   if (board[B1] == EMPTY && board[C1] == EMPTY &&
board[D1] == EMPTY) {
    AddMove(E1, C1);
   }
  }
 } else {
  if (game_list[hply].castle_k1 > 0) {
   if (board[F8] == EMPTY && board[G8] == EMPTY)
    AddMove(E8, G8);
  }
  if (game_list[hply].castle_q1 > 0) {
   if (board[B8] == EMPTY && board[C8] == EMPTY &&
board[D8] == EMPTY)
    AddMove(E8, C8);
  }
 }
}
```

GenCastle() generates castling moves and adds them to the move list. It looks at castling permissions for both the queenside and kingside. If the castling permission is true and the relevant squares are empty then a castling move is added to the list. Castling may still prove to be illegal, due to the king moving out of, into or through check.

GenPawn

sq is the square the pawn is on.

```
function GenPawn(sq) {
 if (board[PawnMove[side][sq]] == EMPTY) {
  AddMove(sq, PawnMove[side][sq]);
  if (rank[side][sq] == 1 && board[PawnDouble[side]
[sq]] == EMPTY)
    AddMove(sq, PawnDouble[side][sq]);
 }
 if (color[PawnCaptureLeft[side][sq]] == xside)
  AddCapture(sq, PawnCaptureLeft[side][sq],
PawnCapScore[board[PawnCaptureLeft[side][sq]]]);
 if (color[PawnCaptureRight[side][sq]] == xside)
  AddCapture(sq, PawnCaptureRight[side][sq],
PawnCapScore[board[PawnCaptureRight[side][sq]]]);
}
```

GenPawn() generates moves and captures for a pawn and adds them to the move list. White pawns may capture left, unless they are on the a-file, (col[square] = 0). White pawns may capture right, unless they are on the h-file, (col[square] = 7).

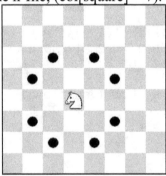

GenKnight

sq is the square the knight is on.

```
function GenKnight(sq) {
 var c = 0;
 var sq2 = KnightMoves[sq][c++];
 while (sq2 > -1) {
  if (color[sq2] == EMPTY) {
   AddMove(sq, sq2);
  } else if (color[sq2] == xside) {
   AddCapture(sq, sq2, KnightCapScore[board[sq2]]);
  }
  sq2 = KnightMoves[sq][c++];
 }
}
```

GenKnight() generates moves and captures for a knight and adds them to the move list. The **KnightMoves[]** lookup table is used.

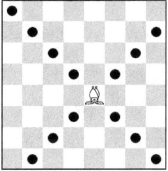

GenBishop

sq is the square the bishop is on. **dir** is the direction it is moving in.

```
function GenBishop(sq, dir) {
 var sq2 = LineMoves[sq][dir];
 while (sq2 > -1) {
  if (color[sq2] != EMPTY) {
   if (color[sq2] == xside) {
    AddCapture(sq, sq2, BishopCapScore[board[sq2]]);
   }
   break;
  }
  AddMove(sq, sq2);
  sq2 = LineMoves[sq2][dir];
 }
}
```

GenBishop() generates moves and captures for a bishop and adds them to the move list. The **LineMoves[]** lookup table is used.

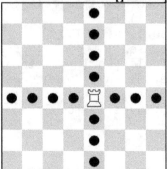

GenRook

sq is the square the rook is on. **dir** is the direction it is moving in.

```
function GenRook(sq, dir) {
 var sq2 = LineMoves[sq][dir];
 while (sq2 > -1) {
  if (color[sq2] != EMPTY) {
   if (color[sq2] == xside) {
    AddCapture(sq, sq2, RookCapScore[board[sq2]]);
   }
   break;
  }
  AddMove(sq, sq2);
  sq2 = LineMoves[sq2][dir];
 }
}
```

GenRook() generates moves and captures for a rook and adds them to the move list. The **LineMoves[]** lookup table is used.

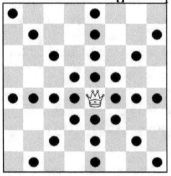

GenQueen

sq is the square the queen is on. **dir** is the direction it is moving in.

```
function GenQueen(sq, dir) {
 var sq2 = LineMoves[sq][dir];
 while (sq2 > -1) {
  if (color[sq2] != EMPTY) {
   if (color[sq2] == xside) {
    AddCapture(sq, sq2, QueenCapScore[board[sq2]]);
   }
   break;
  }
  AddMove(sq, sq2);
  sq2 = LineMoves[sq2][dir];
 }
}
```

GenQueen() generates moves and captures for a queen and adds them to the move list. The **LineMoves[]** lookup table is used.

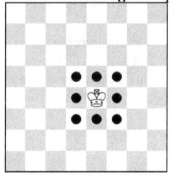

GenKing

sq is the square the king is on.

```
function GenKing(sq) {
 var c = 0;
 var sq2 = KingMoves[sq][c++];
 while (sq2 > -1) {
  if (color[sq2] == EMPTY) {
   AddMove(sq, sq2);
  } else if (color[sq2] == xside) {
   AddCapture(sq, sq2, KingCapScore[board[sq2]]);
```

```
    }
    sq2 = KingMoves[sq][c++];
  }
}
```

GenKing() generates moves and captures for a king and adds them to the move list. Note that if the king is captured it is an illegal move. This means the score is merely the captured pieces X 10. The **KingMoves[]** lookup table is used.

AddMove

from is the from square. **to** is the to square.

```
function AddMove(from, to) {
  move_list[move_count].from = from;
  move_list[move_count].to = to;
  move_list[move_count].score = Hist[from][to];
  move_count++;
}
```

AddMove() adds a non-capturing move to the move list. The **from** and **dest** squares are stored. The score is from the history table. It is the number of times the same move has been the best move so far. This is only an approximation, though it is a lot better than nothing.

AddCapture

from is the from square. **to** is the to square. **score** is the move score.

```
function AddCapture(from, to, score) {
  move_list[move_count].from = from;
  move_list[move_count].to = to;
  move_list[move_count].score = score;
  move_count++;
}
```

AddCapture() adds a capture to the move list. The **from** and **dest** squares are stored. The score is the piece captured X 10 minus the piece capturing. For example, a bishop is 2 and a rook is 3. If a rook takes a bishop the score is 20 - 3 = 17. Captures of the most valuable pieces are searched first.

If more than capture, capture pieces of the same value, the least valuable attacker is searched first.

CAPTURE_SCORE is added to the score so that captures will be searched before non-captures.//

Capture Generation

GenCaptures

```javascript
function GenCaptures() {
 move_count = first_move[ply];
 for (var x = 0; x < 64; x++) {
  if (color[x] == side) {
   switch (board[x]) {
    case P:
     CapPawn(x);
     break;
    case N:
     CapKnight(x);
     break;
    case B:
     CapBishop(x, NE);
     CapBishop(x, SE);
     CapBishop(x, SW);
     CapBishop(x, NW);
     break;
    case R:
     CapRook(x, EAST);
     CapRook(x, SOUTH);
     CapRook(x, WEST);
     CapRook(x, NORTH);
     break;
    case Q:
     CapQueen(x, NE);
     CapQueen(x, SE);
     CapQueen(x, SW);
     CapQueen(x, NW);
     CapQueen(x, EAST);
     CapQueen(x, SOUTH);
     CapQueen(x, WEST);
     CapQueen(x, NORTH);
     break;
    case K:
     CapKing(x);
     break;
    default:
     break;
   }
  }
 }
```

```
}
  first_move[ply + 1] = move_count;
}
```

GenCaptures() generates all captures for one side. It is very similar to **Gen()**.

CapPawn

sq is the square the pawn is on.

```
function CapPawn(sq) {
  if (color[PawnCaptureLeft[side][sq]] == xside)
   AddCapture(sq, PawnCaptureLeft[side][sq],
PawnCapScore[board[PawnCaptureLeft[side][sq]]]);
  if (color[PawnCaptureRight[side][sq]] == xside)
   AddCapture(sq, PawnCaptureRight[side][sq],
PawnCapScore[board[PawnCaptureRight[side][sq]]]);
}
```

CapPawn() generates all captures for a pawn on a given square, by the lookup-tables populated with **SetPawns()**. Pawn captures get a high score because they involve capturing with the weakest unit. Even if the captured piece is defended, the pawn capture will make a material gain.

The white pawn captures **gxf4** and **gxh4** are added to the move list. The from square is **g3** which is 15, while the **dest** squares are 22 and 24.

43

CapKnight

sq is the square the knight is on.

```
function CapKnight(sq) {
 var c = 0;
 var sq2 = KnightMoves[sq][c++];
 while (sq2 > -1) {
  if (color[sq2] == xside) {
   AddCapture(sq, sq2, KnightCapScore[board[sq2]]);
  }
  sq2 = KnightMoves[sq][c++];
 }
}
```

CapKnight() generates all captures for a knight on a given square. Knight captures get the equal 2nd highest score.

CapBishop

sq is the square the bishop is on. **dir** is the direction it is moving in.

```
function CapBishop(sq, dir) {
 var sq2 = LineMoves[sq][dir];
 while (sq2 > -1) {
  if (color[sq2] != EMPTY) {
   if (color[sq2] == xside) {
    AddCapture(sq, sq2, BishopCapScore[board[sq2]]);
   }
   break;
  }
  sq2 = LineMoves[sq2][dir];
 }
}
```

CapBishop() generates all captures for a bishop on a given square. Bishops captures get the equal 2nd highest score, being roughly the same value as a Knight.

CapRook

sq is the square the rook is on. **dir** is the direction it is moving in.

```
function CapRook(sq, dir) {
 var sq2 = LineMoves[sq][dir];
 while (sq2 > -1) {
  if (color[sq2] != EMPTY) {
   if (color[sq2] == xside) {
    AddCapture(sq, sq2, RookCapScore[board[sq2]]);
   }
   break;
  }
  sq2 = LineMoves[sq2][dir];
 }
}
```

CapRook() generates all captures for a rook on a given square.
Rook captures get the 4th highest score.

CapQueen

sq is the square the queen is on. **dir** is the direction it is moving in.

```
function CapQueen(sq, dir) {
 var sq2 = LineMoves[sq][dir];
 while (sq2 > -1) {
  if (color[sq2] != EMPTY) {
   if (color[sq2] == xside) {
    AddCapture(sq, sq2, QueenCapScore[board[sq2]]);
   }
   break;
  }
  sq2 = LineMoves[sq2][dir];
 }
}
```

CapQueen() generates all diagonal captures for a queen on a given
square. Queen captures get the 5th highest score.

CapKing

sq is the square the king is on.

```
function CapKing(sq) {
 var c = 0;
 var sq2 = KingMoves[sq][c++];
 while (sq2 > -1) {
```

```
if (color[sq2] == xside) {
 AddCapture(sq, sq2, KingCapScore[board[sq2]]);
}
sq2 = KingMoves[sq][c++];
}
}
```

CapKing() generates all captures for a king on a given square. King captures get a high score. This is because if it is legal then the captured piece must be undefended.

Attack

LineCheck

s is the side of the moving piece. **sq** is the square the piece starts on. **d** is the direction it is moving in. **p** is the piece being searched for.

```
function LineCheck(s, sq, d, p) {
 sq = LineMoves[sq][d];
 while (sq > -1) {
  if (color[sq] != EMPTY) {
   if (board[sq] == p && color[sq] == s)
    return sq;
   break;
  }
  sq = LineMoves[sq][d];
 }
 return -1;
}
```

LineCheck() searches a line from square **sq**, in direction **d** for the given piece **p** of the given side **s**. It either returns the square the piece is on or -1 if there are none.

LineCheck2

s is the side of the moving piece **d** is the direction it is moving in. **p1** and **p2** are the pieces being searched for.

```
function LineCheck2(s, d, p1, p2) {
 var sq = LineMoves[sq][d];
 while (sq > -1) {
  if (color[sq] != EMPTY) {
   if ((board[sq] == p1 || board[sq] == p2) &&
color[sq] == s)
    return true;
   break;
  }
  sq = LineMoves[sq][d];
 }
```

```
   return false;
}
```

LineCheck2() searches a line in direction **d** for the given pieces **p1** and **p2** of the given side **s**. On diagonals, it searches for bishops and queens, while on ranks or files it searches for rooks and queens. It returns **false** if there are none.

LineCheck3

sq is the start square. **d** is the direction it is moving in. **sq2** is the end square.

```
function LineCheck3(sq, d, sq2) {
 sq = LineMoves[sq][d];
 while (sq > -1) {
  if (color[sq] != EMPTY) {
   if (sq == sq2)
    return true;
   break;
  }
  sq = LineMoves[sq][d];
 }
 return false;
}
```

LineCheck3() searches a line from square **sq** to square **sq2**, in direction **d**. It returns **true** if the line is unblocked and **false** if the line is blocked.

Attack

s is the attacking side. **sq** is the attacked square.

```
function Attack(s, sq) {
 if (color[PawnCaptureLeft[1 - s][sq]] == s &&
  board[PawnCaptureLeft[1 - s][sq]] == P)
  return true;
 if (color[PawnCaptureRight[1 - s][sq]] == s &&
  board[PawnCaptureRight[1 - s][sq]] == P)
  return true;

 var k = 0;
```

```
var sq2 = KnightMoves[sq][0];

while (sq2 > -1) {
  if (color[sq2] == s && board[sq2] == N)
   return true;
  k++;
  sq2 = KnightMoves[sq][k];
}
if (LineCheck2(s, sq, NE, B, Q)) return true;
if (LineCheck2(s, sq, NW, B, Q)) return true;
if (LineCheck2(s, sq, SW, B, Q)) return true;
if (LineCheck2(s, sq, SE, B, Q)) return true;

if (LineCheck2(s, sq, NORTH, R, Q)) return true;
if (LineCheck2(s, sq, SOUTH, R, Q)) return true;
if (LineCheck2(s, sq, EAST, R, Q)) return true;
if (LineCheck2(s, sq, WEST, R, Q)) return true;

if (Math.abs(COL[sq] - COL[Kingloc[s]]) < 2 &&
Math.abs(ROW[sq] - ROW[Kingloc[s]]) < 2)
  return true;

return false;
}
```

Attack() tests whether the given square is attacked or not by the given player. It is mostly used to prevent illegal moves which have left the king in check. It may have other uses.

It first checks for pawn attacks, then for knight attacks followed by line piece attacks and king attacks.

The black rook on **a1** is attacking the white king on **E1**. Because of this **LineCheck2(1,E1,WEST,R,Q)** returns **true**.

LowestAttacker

s is the attacking side. **sq** is the attacked square.

```
function LowestAttacker(s, sq) {
 if (color[PawnCaptureLeft[xside][sq]] == s &&
  board[PawnCaptureLeft[xside][sq]] == P)
  return PawnCaptureLeft[xside][sq];
 if (color[PawnCaptureRight[xside][sq]] == s &&
  board[PawnCaptureRight[xside][sq]] == P)
  return PawnCaptureRight[xside][sq];
 var k = 0;
 var sq2 = KnightMoves[sq][k];
 while (sq2 > -1) {
  if (color[sq2] == s && board[sq2] == N)
   return sq2;
  k++;
  sq2 = KnightMoves[sq][k];
 }
 sq2 = LineCheck(s, sq, NE, B); if (sq2 > -1) return
sq2;
 sq2 = LineCheck(s, sq, NW, B); if (sq2 > -1) return
sq2;
 sq2 = LineCheck(s, sq, SW, B); if (sq2 > -1) return
sq2;
 sq2 = LineCheck(s, sq, SE, B); if (sq2 > -1) return
sq2;
 sq2 = LineCheck(s, sq, NORTH, R); if (sq2 > -1)
return sq2;
 sq2 = LineCheck(s, sq, SOUTH, R); if (sq2 > -1)
return sq2;
 sq2 = LineCheck(s, sq, EAST, R); if (sq2 > -1) return
sq2;
 sq2 = LineCheck(s, sq, WEST, R); if (sq2 > -1) return
sq2;
 sq2 = LineCheck(s, sq, NORTH, Q); if (sq2 > -1)
return sq2;
 sq2 = LineCheck(s, sq, SOUTH, Q); if (sq2 > -1)
return sq2;
 sq2 = LineCheck(s, sq, EAST, Q); if (sq2 > -1) return
sq2;
 sq2 = LineCheck(s, sq, WEST, Q); if (sq2 > -1) return
sq2;
 sq2 = LineCheck(s, sq, NE, Q); if (sq2 > -1) return
sq2;
 sq2 = LineCheck(s, sq, NW, Q); if (sq2 > -1) return
```

```
sq2;
 sq2 = LineCheck(s, sq, SW, Q); if (sq2 > -1) return
sq2;
 sq2 = LineCheck(s, sq, SE, Q); if (sq2 > -1) return
sq2;
 if (Math.abs(COL[sq] - COL[Kingloc[s]]) < 2 &&
Math.abs(ROW[sq] - ROW[Kingloc[s]]) < 2)
   return Kingloc[s];
 return -1;
}
```

LowestAttacker() returns the square the weakest attacker is on. From weakest to strongest, these are pawn, knight, bishop, rook, queen and king. If there is no attacker -1 is returned. The basic idea is that if several pieces can capture on a square, it is often good to capture with the weakest available piece.

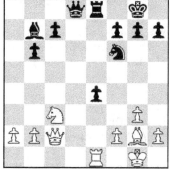

White is attacking the black pawn on e4 with a knight, bishop, rook and queen. The knight is the piece with the lowest value so **LowestAttacker()** returns the square the knight is on, which is 18 (C3 in algebraic).

IsCheck

s is the moving side. **p** is the moving piece. **sq** is the square the piece is on. **k** is the square the opposing king is on.

```
function IsCheck(s, p, sq, k) {
 if (p == P) {
  if (PawnCaptureLeft[s][sq] == k)
   return true;
  if (PawnCaptureRight[s][sq] == k)
```

```
   return true;
  return false;
 }
 if (p == N) {
  var c = 0;
  var sq2 = KnightMoves[sq][0];
  while (sq2 > -1) {
   if (KnightMoves[sq][c] == k)
    return true;
   c++;
   sq2 = KnightMoves[sq][c];
  }
  return false;
 }
 if (p == B || p == Q) {
  if (NE_DIAG[sq] == NE_DIAG[k]) {
   if (sq < k && LineCheck3(sq, NE, k)) return true;
   else if (LineCheck3(sq, SE, k)) return true;
  }
  if (NW_DIAG[sq] == NW_DIAG[k]) {
   if (sq < k && LineCheck3(sq, NW, k)) return true;
   else if (LineCheck3(sq, SW, k)) return true;
  }
 }
 if (p == R || p == Q) {
  if (COL[sq] == COL[k]) {
   if (sq < k && LineCheck3(sq, NORTH, k)) return
true;
   else if (LineCheck3(sq, SOUTH, k)) return true;
  }
  if (ROW[sq] == ROW[k]) {
   if (sq < k && LineCheck3(sq, EAST, k)) {
    return true;
   }
   else if (LineCheck3(sq, WEST, k)) return true;
  }
 }
 return false;
}
```

IsCheck() tests to see if the current move gives check or not. It returns **false** if not.

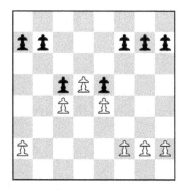

This a pawn skeleton from a game position. The score will be influenced by the white passed pawn on **d5** and isolated pawn on **a2**. The pawn position and score will be stored in the pawn hash table. This pawn position may be the same many times in the search. In those cases, the stored scores will be used instead of using **EvalPawns()**.

Update

There are three functions that are used to update the position, whenever it is changed by **MakeMove()** or **TakeBack()**.

UpdatePiece

s is the moving side. **p** is the moving piece. **from** is the from square. **to** is the to square.

```
function UpdatePiece(s, p, from, to) {
 AddKey(s, p, from);
 AddKey(s, p, to);
 board[to] = p;
 color[to] = s;
 board[from] = EMPTY;
 color[from] = EMPTY;
 Table_score[s] -= square_score[s][p][from];
 Table_score[s] += square_score[s][p][to];
 bit_pieces[s][p] &= not_mask[from];
 bit_pieces[s][p] |= mask[to];
 if (p == P) {
  AddPawnKey(s, from);
  AddPawnKey(s, to);
 } else if (p == K)
  Kingloc[s] = to;
}
```

UpdatePiece() updates information when a unit is moved.

- **currentkey** and **currentlock** are updated.
- The board is updated.
- The table score is modified by the scores of the **from** and **dest** squares.
- **bit_pieces[]** is updated.
- The pawn keys are updated if the moving piece is a pawn.
- If the moving piece is a king, **Kingloc[]** is updated.

RemovePiece

s is the side of the removed piece. **p** is the removed piece. **sq** is the square the piece is on.

```
function RemovePiece(s, p, sq) {
 AddKey(s, p, sq);
 board[sq] = EMPTY;
 color[sq] = EMPTY;
 Table_score[s] -= square_score[s][p][sq];
 bit_pieces[s][p] &= not_mask[sq];
 if (p == P)
   AddPawnKey(s, sq);
}
```

RemovePiece() updates information when a unit is removed.

- The board is updated. This happens when there is a capture or a promotion.
- The table score is modified by the scores of the given square.
- **bit_pieces[]** is updated.

AddPiece

s is the side of the piece. **p** is the added piece. **sq** is the square the piece is on.

```
function AddPiece(s, p, sq) {
 AddKey(s, p, sq);
 board[sq] = p;
 color[sq] = s;
 Table_score[s] += square_score[s][p][sq];
 bit_pieces[s][p] |= mask[sq];
 if (p == P)
   AddPawnKey(s, sq);
}
```

AddPiece() updates information when a unit is added. The board is updated. The table score is modified by the score of the given square. **AddPiece()** is used when a position is initially set up. This also happens when a capture is taken back or when a pawn is promoted.

MakeMove

from is the from square. **to** is the to square.

```
function MakeMove(from, to) {
// Handle castling moves
if (Math.abs(COL[from] - COL[to]) == 2 &&
board[from] == K) {
 if (Attack(xside, from) || Attack(xside, to))
  return false;
 if (to == G1) {//White kingside castling.
  if (Attack(1, F1))
   return false;
  UpdatePiece(0, K, E1, G1);
  UpdatePiece(0, R, H1, F1);
  game_list[hply].castle_k0 = 0;
  game_list[hply].castle_q0 = 0;
 }
 else if (to == C1) {//White queenside castling.
  if (Attack(1, D1))
   return false;
  UpdatePiece(0, K, E1, C1);
  UpdatePiece(0, R, A1, D1);
  game_list[hply].castle_k0 = 0;
  game_list[hply].castle_q0 = 0;
 }
 else if (to == G8) {//Black kingside castling.
  if (Attack(0, F8))
   return false;
  UpdatePiece(1, K, E8, G8);
  UpdatePiece(1, R, H8, F8);
  game_list[hply].castle_k1 = 0;
  game_list[hply].castle_q1 = 0;
 }
 else if (to == C8) {//Black queenside castling.
  if (Attack(0, D8))
   return false;
  UpdatePiece(1, K, E8, C8);
  UpdatePiece(1, R, A8, D8);
  game_list[hply].castle_k1 = 0;
  game_list[hply].castle_q1 = 0;
 }
 game_list[hply].from = from;
 game_list[hply].to = to;
```

```
    game_list[hply].capture = EMPTY;
    game_list[hply].fifty = 0;
    game_list[hply].hash = currentkey;
    game_list[hply].lock = currentlock;
    game_list[hply].start_piece = K;
    ply++;
    hply++;
    game_list[hply].castle_q0 = game_list[hply -
1].castle_q0;
    game_list[hply].castle_q1 = game_list[hply -
1].castle_q1;
    game_list[hply].castle_k0 = game_list[hply -
1].castle_k0;
    game_list[hply].castle_k1 = game_list[hply -
1].castle_k1;
    side ^= 1;
    xside ^= 1;
    return true;
  }
  // Store game state for undoing later
  StoreMoveData(from, to);
  if (board[to] != EMPTY || board[from] == P)
   fifty = 0;
  else
   fifty++;
  // Handle en passant
  if (board[from] == P && board[to] == EMPTY &&
COL[from] != COL[to]) {
    if (side == 0)
     RemovePiece(xside, P, to - 8);
    else
     RemovePiece(xside, P, to + 8);
  }
  else if (board[to] != EMPTY) {
    // Capture move
    RemovePiece(xside, board[to], to);
  }
  if (to == A1 || from == A1)//Rook has moved or has
been captured.
    game_list[hply].castle_q0 = 0;
  else if (to == H1 || from == H1)
    game_list[hply].castle_k0 = 0;
  else if (from == E1) {//King has moved.
    game_list[hply].castle_q0 = 0;
    game_list[hply].castle_k0 = 0;
  }
  if (to == A8 || from == A8)
```

```
   game_list[hply].castle_q1 = 0;
 else if (to == H8 || from == H8)
  game_list[hply].castle_k1 = 0;
 else if (from == E8) {
  game_list[hply].castle_q1 = 0;
  game_list[hply].castle_k1 = 0;
 }
 // Handle pawn promotion
 if (board[from] == P && (ROW[to] == 0 || ROW[to] ==
7)) {
  RemovePiece(side, P, from);
  AddPiece(side, Q, to);
  game_list[hply].promote = Q;
 }
 else {
  game_list[hply].promote = 0;
  UpdatePiece(side, board[from], from, to);
 }
 // Change turns
 side ^= 1;
 xside ^= 1;
 // Check if move puts own king in check
 if (Attack(side, Kingloc[xside])) {
  TakeBack();
  return false;
 }
 return true;
}
```

MakeMove() updates information when a move is made.

- If the king moves 2 squares it must be *castling*. If the king is not in check and doesn't move through check, the matching rook move is made.
- The game_list information is updated.
- If there is a capture or pawn move then the fifty move count is reset to zero.
- If a pawn changes files and the destination square is empty then it is an *en passant* capture.
- Castling permissions are changed if needed.
- Either a promotion or a normal move is made.
- If the move leaves the king in check the move is taken back. This includes moving a piece pinned to the king.

1...Nxd4 is added to the move list. It is played with **MakeMove**, however after moving, the black king is attacked. 1...Nxd4 is taken back and the next move is examined.

StoreMoveData

from is the from square. **to** is the to square.

```
function StoreMoveData(from, to) {
game_list[hply].from = from;
game_list[hply].to = to;
game_list[hply].capture = board[to];
game_list[hply].fifty = fifty;
game_list[hply].hash = currentkey;
game_list[hply].lock = currentlock;
game_list[hply].start_piece = board[from];
ply++;
hply++;
// Copy castle rights from previous move
game_list[hply].castle_q0 = game_list[hply -
1].castle_q0;
game_list[hply].castle_q1 = game_list[hply -
1].castle_q1;
game_list[hply].castle_k0 = game_list[hply -
1].castle_k0;
game_list[hply].castle_k1 = game_list[hply -
1].castle_k1;
}
```

TakeBack

```
function TakeBack() {
 // Switch back sides
 side ^= 1;
 xside ^= 1;
 // Decrease ply and history ply
 ply--;
 hply--;
 const from = game_list[hply].from;
 const to = game_list[hply].to;
 const capture = game_list[hply].capture;
 // Restore the fifty-move rule counter
 fifty = game_list[hply].fifty;

 // Handle en passant undo
 if (board[to] === P && game_list[hply].capture ==
EMPTY && COL[from] !== COL[to]) {
  UpdatePiece(side, P, to, from);
  if (side === 0) {
   AddPiece(xside, P, to - 8);  // Restore captured
pawn for black
  } else {
   AddPiece(xside, P, to + 8);  // Restore captured
pawn for white
  }
  return;
 }
 if (game_list[hply].start_piece == P && (ROW[to] == 0
|| ROW[to] == 7)) {
  AddPiece(side, P, from);
  RemovePiece(side, board[to], to);
 }
 else
  UpdatePiece(side, board[to], to, from);
 // Restore captured piece if any
 if (capture !== EMPTY) {
  AddPiece(xside, capture, to);
 }
 // Handle castling undo
 if (Math.abs(COL[from] - COL[to]) === 2 &&
board[from] === K) {
  UndoCastling(to);
 }
}
```

TakeBack() updates information when a move is taken back.

- An *en passant* or promotion is taken back, otherwise a normal move is taken back.
- If a piece has been captured it is added to the board.
- If the move was castling then the move of the matching rook is taken back.

UndoCastling

to is the to square of the moving king.

```
function UndoCastling(to) {
 if (to === G1) { //White kingside castling.
  UpdatePiece(0, R, F1, H1);
  game_list[hply].castle_k0 = 1;
 } else if (to === C1) { //White queenside castling.
  UpdatePiece(0, R, D1, A1);
  game_list[hply].castle_q0 = 1;
 } else if (to === G8) { //Black kingside castling.
  UpdatePiece(1, R, F8, H8);
  game_list[hply].castle_k1 = 1;
 } else if (to === C8) { //Black queenside castling.
  UpdatePiece(1, R, D8, A8);
  game_list[hply].castle_q1 = 1;
 }
}
```

UndoCastling() returns the castling rook to its original square. Note that this has already been done for the king.

MakeRecapture

from is the from square. **to** is the to square.

```
function MakeRecapture(from, to) {
 game_list[hply].from = from;
 game_list[hply].to = to;
 game_list[hply].capture = board[to];
 ply++;
 hply++;
 board[to] = board[from];
 color[to] = color[from];
```

```
 board[from] = EMPTY;
 color[from] = EMPTY;
 if (board[to] == K)
  Kingloc[side] = to;
 side ^= 1;
 xside ^= 1;
 if (Attack(side, Kingloc[xside])) {
  UnMakeRecapture();
  return false;
 }
 return true;
}
```

MakeRecapture() updates information when a capture is made.

- **game_list[]** is updated.
- The board is updated.
- If a king moves then the king location(KingLoc[]) is updated.
- **side** and **xside** are flipped.
- If the move leaves the king in check the move is taken back.

Because it only deals with captures, updating castling permissions, hash keys and locks, and **fifty** are not needed to be updated.

UnMakeRecapture

```
function UnMakeRecapture() {
 side ^= 1;
 xside ^= 1;
 --ply;
 --hply;
 var from = game_list[hply].from;
 var to = game_list[hply].to;
 board[from] = board[to];
 color[from] = color[to];
 board[to] = game_list[hply].capture;
 color[to] = xside;
 if (board[from] == K)
  Kingloc[side] = from;
}
```

UnMakeRecapture() updates information when a capture is taken back.

- **side**, **xside**, **ply** and **hply** are changed.
- The board is updated.
- If a king moves then the king's location is updated.

Search

Think

```
function Think() {
 root_from = 0;
 root_to = 0;
 var score;
 ply = 0;
 nodes = 0;
 first_move[0] = 0;
 NewPosition();
 Gen();
 var count = 0;
 for (var i = first_move[ply]; i < first_move[ply +
1]; i++) {
  if (!MakeMove(move_list[i].from, move_list[i].to))
   continue;
  TakeBack();
  count++;
  if (count > 1)
   break;
 }
/* We see if there is only one legal move. If so, the
engine can move instantly.
*/
 if (count == 1)
  max_depth = 1;
/* If there is only one legal, we are only searching
to a depth of one ply.
*/
 for (var x1 = 0; x1 < 64; x1++) {
  for (var y1 = 0; y1 < 64; y1++)
   Hist[x1][y1] = 0;
 }
 const start = Date.now();
/* The start time is found.
*/
 for (var i = 1; i <= max_depth; i++) {
  currentkey = GetKey();
  currentlock = GetLock();
  deep = 0;
  score = Search(-10000, 10000, i);
  if (score > 9998)
```

```
    postMessage("add=Checkmate!
");
  else
    postMessage("add=" + i + " deepest " + deep + " " +
score + " " + " " + nodes + "
");
  if (LookUp(side))
    DisplayPV(i);
  if (score > 9000 || score < -9000)
    break;
  if (max_time > 0 && Number(Date.now() - start) > 0
&& Number(Date.now() - start) > max_time * 1000) {
    max_depth = i;
    break;
  }
 }
}
```

Think() selects a move for a computer player. The history table is
cleared. A loop starts at one ply continuing to the **max_depth** or
until **max_time** has been exceeded. **Search()** is called during each
iteration of the loop. Some information is displayed with each
iteration. If the search finds mate, the loop ends. The move played
(root_from to root_to) is posted to board.html.

DisplayPV

```
function DisplayPV(i) {
 var text = "";
 for (var x = 0; x < i; x++) {
  if (LookUp(side) == false)
   break;
  text += LongAlgebraic(board[hash_from], hash_from,
hash_to, board[hash_to]) + " ";
  MakeMove(hash_from, hash_to);
 }
 while (ply)
  TakeBack();
 postMessage("add= PV " + i + "\\" + deep + " " +
text);
}
```

The *principal variation* or PV is the best line of play for both sides,
which has been found so far. **DisplayPV()** searches the hash table

for the best move. The move is played and posted. A loop is continued until no more moves can be found. All the moves are taken back. The principal variation is displayed. This is called by **Think()**.

The best line of play for both sides in this position (i.e. the principal variation) is **1.Nxe5 dxe5 2. Qxg4**. 1...Bxd1? 2.Bxf7+ Ke7 3.Nd5# is a critical variation, but not the principal variation. The JS engine finds 1.Nxe5! very quickly.

Search

alpha is the best score of the side to move. It starts at -10,000 and increases. **beta** is the best score of the other side to move. It starts at 10,000 and reduces. **depth** is the number of plies left to search. It usually is reduced by one with each call to **Search()**, unless there is an extension or reduction.

```
function Search(alpha, beta, depth) {
 if (ply && Reps2())
  return 0;
 /* If the position is repeated, there is no need to
search further.
 */
 if (bit_pieces[0][P] == 0 && bit_pieces[1][P] == 0 &&
Table_score[0] < 400 && Table_score[1] < 400)
  return 0;
 /* If neither side has mating material, there is no
need to search further.
 */
 if (depth < 1)
  return CaptureSearch(alpha, beta);
```

```
/* If there is no depth left, a CaptureSearch is
performed.
 */
 nodes++;
 if (ply > MAX_PLY - 2)
  return Eval();
 var InCheck = 0, Check = 0;
 if (Attack(xside, Kingloc[side])) {
  InCheck = 1;
 }
 /* We see if the player to move is in check.
 */
 Gen();
 if (LookUp(side))
  SetHashMove();
 /* If the position is found in the hashtable, the
hash move is found and given the highest score.
 */
 var bestmove = new Move();
 var bestscore = -10001;
 var count = 0;
 var d;
 var score = 0;
 var zero_flag = 0;
 var from, to;
 var e = 10000, diff = 0;
 for (var i = first_move[ply]; i < first_move[ply +
1]; i++) {
  if (zero_flag == 0) {
   Sort(i);
   if (move_list[i].score == 0)
    zero_flag = 1;
  }
  from = move_list[i].from;
  to = move_list[i].to;
  if (InCheck == 0)
   Check = (IsCheck(side, board[from], to,
Kingloc[xside]))
  else
   Check = 0;
  /* Is the move played check?
  */
  if (Check) {
   d = depth;
   /* Normally depth is decremented by one, with each
depth.
   However, checks are moves of interest, so we extend
```

```
the search by one by leaving depth unchanged.
  */
 }
 else {
  if (move_list[i].score > 0 || ply < 2 || InCheck ==
1)
   d = depth - 1;
   /* This is the default. depth is reduced by one.
   */
  else
   d = depth - 2;
   /* The search depth is reduced by two. This is a
reduction.
   */
 }
 if (d < 2 && count > 0 && Check == 0 && board[to] ==
EMPTY &&
  !(board[from] == P && rank[side][from] == EMPTY)) {
  if (e == 10000)
  e = Eval();
  if (board[from] == K && bit_pieces[xside][Q] == 0)
   diff = King_endgame[side][to] - King_endgame[side]
[from];
  else
   diff = square_score[side][board[from]][to] -
square_score[side][board[from]][from];
  if (e + diff < alpha) {
   nodes++;
   continue;
  }
 }
 /* This block performs frontier pruning. At the end
of the search (i.e. depth == 1),
  moves that have no chance of reaching alpha are
ignored.
  */
 if (!MakeMove(from, to))
  continue;
 /* The move is made. It might be illegal, usually as
a result of moving a piece pinned to the king.
  In that case the move is taken back and ignored.
  */
 count++;
 score = -Search(-beta, -alpha, d);
 TakeBack();
 /* The move is taken back.
  */
```

```
  if (score > bestscore) {
    bestscore = score;
    bestmove = move_list[i];
    if (ply == 0) {
      root_from = from;
      root_to = to;
      root_score = score;
    }
  }
  if (score > alpha) {
    if (score >= beta) {
      if (board[to] == EMPTY)
        Hist[from][to] += depth;
      /* If the move is not a capture, we add it to the
history table.
      */
      AddHash(side, move_list[i]);
      /* The move is added to the hashtable.
      */
      return beta;
    }
    alpha = score;
  }
}
if (count == 0) {
  if (Attack(xside, Kingloc[side]))
    return -10000 + ply;
  else
    return 0;
}
/* If there are no legal moves, it is checkmate or
stalemate.
*/
if (fifty >= 100)
  return 0;
/* If 50 moves by both sides have been played without
a pawn move or capture, it is a drawn position.
*/
AddHash(side, bestmove);
/* The best move is added to the hashtable.
*/
return alpha;
}
```

Search() executes the main search loop. If the position is repeated then a score of zero is returned. If the depth is less than one or ply is too deep, then a score is returned. The node count (number of positions searched) is incremented. It is determined if the player to move is in check or not.

Moves are generated. If the position is in the hash table, then the hash move is given the highest score. All possible moves are looped through. The move is made.

The depth is calculated. There is a recursive call to **Search()**. The move is taken back. If the score is greater than the current **bestscore**, then **bestmove** is updated. If the score is greater than **alpha** and greater than or equal to **beta** then a cutoff is created and the position and move are added to the hash table.

If there are no legal moves then it is either checkmate or stalemate. If 50 moves are played without a pawn move or capture then it is a drawn position. The best move is stored in the hash table and **alpha** is returned.

CaptureSearch

alpha and **beta** are passed to **CaptureSearch()** as they are to **Search()**.

```
function CaptureSearch(alpha, beta) {
 nodes++;
 var eval = Eval();
 if (eval > alpha) {
  if (eval >= beta)
    return beta;
  alpha = eval;
 } else if (eval + 900 < alpha)
  return alpha;
 var score = 0, bestmove = 0; best = 0;
 GenCaptures();
 for (var i = first_move[ply]; i < first_move[ply +
1]; i++) {
  Sort(i);
  if (eval + piece_value[board[move_list[i].to]] <
alpha)
    continue;
  score = ReCaptureSearch(move_list[i].from,
```

```
move_list[i].to);
  if (score > best) {
    best = score;
    bestmove = i;
  }
}
if (best > 0)
 eval += best;
if (eval > alpha) {
 if (eval >= beta) {
  if (best > 0)
   AddHash(side, move_list[bestmove]);
  return beta;
 }
 return eval;
}
return alpha;
}
```

CaptureSearch() evaluates the position to see if a cutoff is reached. If the difference between the score and **alpha** is more than a queen, then no capture search is done. This is because no capture can bring the score up to **alpha**.

Captures are generated and looped through. Insufficient captures are ignored. A score is calculated by examining recaptures on the same square. The **bestscore** is tested if see if it causes a cutoff.

ReCaptureSearch

The **attacker** is the from square of the piece making the initial capture. **sq** is the square where captures and recaptures happen.

```
function ReCaptureSearch(attacker, sq) {
 var lowest;
 var taker = 0;
 var captures = 0;
 var score = [0, 0, 0, 0, 0, 0, 0, 0, 0, 0, 0, 0];
 score[0] = piece_value[board[sq]];
 score[1] = piece_value[board[attacker]];
 var total_score = 0;
 while (taker < 10) {
  if (!MakeRecapture(attacker, sq))
   break;
```

```
  captures++;
  nodes++;
  taker++;
  lowest = LowestAttacker(side, sq);
  if (lowest > -1) {
    score[taker + 1] = piece_value[board[lowest]];
    if (score[taker] > score[taker - 1] + score[taker +
1]) {
      taker--;
      break;
    }
  } else
    break;
  attacker = lowest;
 }
 while (taker > 1) {
  if (score[taker - 1] >= score[taker - 2])
   taker -= 2;
  else
   break;
 }
 for (var x = 0; x < taker; x++) {
  if (x % 2 == 0)
    total_score += score[x];
  else
    total_score -= score[x];
 }
 if (ply > deep)
  deep = ply;//Is this the deepest variation?
 while (captures) {
  UnMakeRecapture();
  captures--;
 }
 return total_score;
}
```

ReCaptureSearch() generates recaptures on a given square. A loop continues while there are viable captures and recaptures on the same square. This is called by **CaptureSearch()**.

FM Bill Jordan

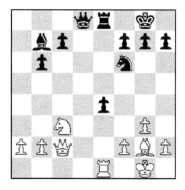

White is attacking the black pawn on e4 with a knight, bishop, rook and queen while Black is defending with knight, bishop and rook.

- score[0] is initially 100, which the value of the black pawn.
- score[1] is 300, the value of the white knight (attacker).
- Black recaptures with the knight.
- **lowest** is the next lowest white taker, which is the bishop.
- This continues until Black cannot recapture any more.
- The total score is calculated by adding the values of the captured pieces.
- All the captures are unmade.
- The total score is returned.

Reps

```
function Reps() {
 var r = 0;
 for (var i = hply - 4; i >= hply - fifty; i -= 2) {
  if (game_list[i].hash == currentkey &&
game_list[i].lock == currentlock)
   r++;
 }
 return r;
}
```

Reps() counts how many times the current position has been repeated during the game. It is not used during the search. It checks if any of the previous positions (which the same side to move) have the same key and lock. If they do then they are the same

73

position. If the position is repeated 3 times it is a draw. This is called by **GetResult()**.

Reps2

```
function Reps2() {
  for (var i = hply - 4; i >= hply - fifty; i -= 2) {
   if (game_list[i].hash == currentkey &&
game_list[i].lock == currentlock)
    return 1;
  }
  return 0;
}
```

Reps2() tests whether the current position has been repeated during the search. It checks if any of the previous positions (which the same side to move) have the same key and lock. If they do then, they are the same position and the search of that line is ended. This is called by **Search()**.

Sort

from is the point in the move list that the search in the move list starts. **Sort()** can be relatively slow, though leads to a slight speed increase.

```
function Sort(from) {
  var bestscore = 0;
  var bestmove = from;
  for (var i = from; i < first_move[ply + 1]; i++)
   if (move_list[i].score > bestscore) {
    bestscore = move_list[i].score;
    bestmove = i;
   }
  var temp = move_list[from];
  move_list[from] = move_list[bestmove];
  move_list[bestmove] = temp;
}
```

Sort() searches the move list for the move with the highest score. This move is moved to the top of the list. The earlier a cutoff is made, the less positions that need to be searched. Searching moves that are most likely to cause a cutoff first, helps an engine search deeper. Moves are searched in this order.

- Move from the hash table, if there is one.
- Captures, in order of most valuable captured then least valuable attacker.
- History moves. These are non-capturing moves that have caused cutoffs in other positions.
- All other moves.

This is called by **Search()** and **CaptureSearch()**.

SetHashMove

```
function SetHashMove() {
 for (var x = first_move[ply]; x < first_move[ply +
1]; x++) {
  if (move_list[x].from == hash_from &&
move_list[x].to == hash_to) {
   move_list[x].score = HASH_SCORE;
   return;
  }
 }
}
```

SetHashMove() searches all moves to see which move is the hash move. That move is given a high score so that it will be examined first. This is called by **Search()**.

Evaluation

Eval

```
function Eval() {
 var score = Table_score[0] - Table_score[1];
 if (GetHashPawns() == -1) {
  score += EvalPawns();
 } else {
  score += GetHashPawns();
 }
 if (bit_pieces[1][Q] == 0)
  score += King_endgame[0][Kingloc[0]];
 else {
  if (ROW[Kingloc[0]] == 0 && color[PawnMove[0]
[Kingloc[0]]] == 0 && board[PawnMove[0][Kingloc[0]]]
== P)
   score += 10;
 }
 if (bit_pieces[0][Q] == 0)
  score -= King_endgame[1][Kingloc[1]];
 else {
  if (ROW[Kingloc[1]] == 7 && color[PawnMove[1]
[Kingloc[1]]] == 1 && board[PawnMove[1][Kingloc[1]]]
== P)
   score -= 10;
 }
 if (side == 0)
  return score;
 else
  return -score;
}
```

Eval() evaluates a position. It will return a single number, which is somewhere between 10,000 and -10,000. A score of 0 represents an equal position. It starts with the table scores, which are incrementally updated with **MakeMove()** or **TakeBack()**.

If the position is not in the pawn hash table then a score is calculated for the pawns and stored in the pawn hash table. Otherwise, the pawn hash table score is used.

If the opponent does not have a queen, then the king endgame score is added. If the opponent has a queen, then there is a bonus of 10 if the king is on one of the first 2 ranks on its side of the board and there is a pawn of the same colour in front of it.

If it is White to move, the score is returned. If it is Black to move, the situation is reversed and -score is returned.

EvalPawns

```
function EvalPawns() {
 var score = 0;
 var s;//side
 for (var x = A2; x < A8; x++) {
  if (board[x] == P) {
   s = color[x];
   if (!(mask_passed[s][x] & bit_pieces[s ^ 1][P]))
    score += Passed[s][x];
   if ((mask_isolated[x] & bit_pieces[s][P]) == 0)
    score += ISOLATED_SCORE[s];
  }
 }
 AddHashPawns(score);
 return score;
}
```

EvalPawns() scores the position of all pawns. A loop traverses all pawns. Pawns cannot be on the first and last ranks so the loop ignores squares less than A2 or greater than H7.

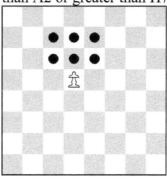

If there are no opposing pawns in the passed pawn mask, then the passed pawn square score is added.

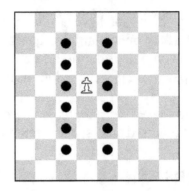

An isolated pawn is weaker than other pawns, because it cannot be defended by another pawn. If there are no friendly pawns in the isolated pawn mask, then the isolated pawn score is added.

Hash Tables

```
const HASH_SIZE = 500000;
const HASH_TABLE_SIZE = 1048576;
const MAX_PAWN_HASH = 65536;
const PAWN_HASH_SIZE = 32768;
/*Array sizes.
*/
var whitehash = new Create2DArray(6, 64);
var blackhash = new Create2DArray(6, 64);
var whitelock = new Create2DArray(6, 64);
var blacklock = new Create2DArray(6, 64);
var piecehash = new Create3DArray(2, 6, 64);
var piecelock = new Create3DArray(2, 6, 64);
var pawnhash = new Create2DArray(2, 64);
var pawnlock = new Create2DArray(2, 64);
var hashpawns = new Create2DArray(2, MAX_PAWN_HASH);
var white_hashtable = [];
var black_hashtable = [];
var hashpawns = [];

function hashp() {
var hashlock = 0;
var from = 0;
var to = 0;
}
function hashpawn() {
var hashlock = 0;
var score = 0;
}
var clashes = 0, collisions = 0;
var hash_from, hash_to;// The move from the hash
table.
```

SetHashTables

```
function SetHashTables() {
for (x = 0; x < HASHSIZE + 100000; x++) {
  white_hashtable.push(new hashp());
  black_hashtable.push(new hashp());
  }
  for (var x = 0; x < MAXPAWNHASH; x++) {
  hashpawns.push(new hashpawn());
  }
```

}

SetHashTables() creates the multi-dimensional arrays representing the hash tables.

RandomizeHashTables

```
function RandomizeHashTables() {
for (var s = 0; s < 2; s++) {
  for (var x = 0; x < 64; x++) {
  pawnhash[s][x] = Random(PAWNHASHSIZE);
  pawnlock[s][x] = Random(PAWNHASHSIZE);
  }
  }
  for (var s = 0; s < 2; s++) {
  for (var p = 0; p < 6; p++) {
  for (var x = 0; x < 64; x++) {
    piecehash[s][p][x] = Random(HASHSIZE);
    piecelock[s][p][x] = Random(HASHSIZE);
  }
  }
  }
}
```

RandomizeHashTables() fills the hash tables with random numbers.

Random

x is the upper limit of the random number.

```
function Random(x) {
return Math.floor(Math.random() * x);
}
```

Random() generates a random integer between 0 and x. It is used to seed the hash tables.

AddHash

s is the current side. **m** is themove stored in the hash table.

```
function AddHash(s, m) {
  if (s == 0) {
   white_hashtable[currentkey].hashlock = currentlock;
   white_hashtable[currentkey].from = m.from;
   white_hashtable[currentkey].to = m.to;
  } else {
   black_hashtable[currentkey].hashlock = currentlock;
   black_hashtable[currentkey].from = m.from;
   black_hashtable[currentkey].to = m.to;
  }
}
```

AddHash() is called whenever a move causes a **beta** cutoff.

AddHash() adds the move that caused the cutoff, **m** to the hash table of the given side. If it is white to move then **white_hashtable** is used, if it is black to move then **black_hashtable** is used. **currentkey** is used as the array index. Any entry already there is overwritten.

AddKey

s is the current side. **p** is the piece. **x** is the square.

```
function AddKey(s, p, x) {
currentkey ^= piecehash[s][p][x];
currentlock ^= piecelock[s][p][x];
}
```

AddKey() alters **currentkey** and **currentlock** whenever the position changes. It uses the side, piece and square. This is done by using bitwise XOR operations with the matching table entries.

GetKey

```
function GetKey() {
  var key = 0;
  for (var x = 0; x < 64; x++) {
  if (board[x] != EMPTY) {
  key ^= piecehash[color[x]][board[x]][x];
  }
}
return key;
```

```
}
```

GetKey() calculates the key for the current position in a similar way to **GetLock()**.

GetLock

```
function GetLock() {
  var lock = 0;
  for (var x = 0; x < 64; x++) {
  if (board[x] != EMPTY) {
  lock ^= piecelock[color[x]][board[x]][x];
  }
  }
  return lock;
}
```

GetLock() calculates the lock for the current position. It is better if **lock** is a 64 bit integer. This can done using the function **BigInt()**. However, this is not used as Safari does not support it. If you run the engine with a different browser then **BigInt** may work.

LookUp

s is the current side.

```
function LookUp(s) {
  if (s == 0) {
  if (white_hashtable[currentkey].hashlock !=
currentlock)
  return false;
  hash_from = white_hashtable[currentkey].from;
  hash_to = white_hashtable[currentkey].to;
  } else {
  if (black_hashtable[currentkey].hashlock !=
currentlock)
  return false;
  hash_from = black_hashtable[currentkey].from;
  hash_to = black_hashtable[currentkey].to;
  }
  return true;
}
```

LookUp() checks to see if there is an entry in the hash table for the current lock and side. If so it stores the move in the hash table in the global variables **hash_from** and **hash_to** and returns **true**.

In this position, **1.Ke6** wins the pawn on d6 and soon the game. 1.Ke6 caused a **beta** cutoff, therefore this position was stored in the hash table along with the move Ke6. Whenever this position arrives due to a transposition of moves or it a later iteration in **Think()**, **LookUp()** will find it in the hash table. The move Ke6 will be searched first. Note that a move causing a beta cutoff does not have to be a winning move, it just has to be the move the engine thinks is the best, at that moment.

Pawn Hash Tables

GetPawnKey

```
function GetPawnKey() {
  var key = 0;
  for (var x = 0; x < 64; x++) {
  if (board[x] == P) {
  key ^= pawnhash[color[x]][x];
  }
  }
  return key;
}
```

GetPawnKey() calculates the pawn key for the current position. This is used with the pawn hash tables.

GetPawnLock

```
  function GetPawnLock() {
var key = 0;
 for (var x = 0; x < 64; x++) {
  if (board[x] == P) {
  key ^= pawnlock[color[x]][x];
  }
  }
  return key;
}
```

GetPawnLock() calculates the pawn lock for the current position. This is used with the pawn hash tables.

AddPawnKey

s is the side. **x** is the square.

```
function AddPawnKey(s, x) {
  currentpawnkey ^= pawnhash[s][x];
  currentpawnlock ^= pawnlock[s][x];
}
```

AddPawnKey() updates **currentpawnkey** and **currentpawnlock** whenever the pawn position changes. This is used with the pawn hash tables.

AddHashPawns

score is the pawn structure value of the current position.

```
function AddHashPawns(score) {
  hashpawns[currentpawnkey].hashlock =
currentpawnlock;
  hashpawns[currentpawnkey].score = score;
}
```

AddHashPawns() updates the entry in the pawn hash table which matches the **currentpawnkey**.

GetHashPawns

```
function GetHashPawns() {
  if (hashpawns[currentpawnkey].hashlock ==
currentpawnlock)
  return hashpawns[currentpawnkey].score;
  return -1;
}
```

GetHashPawns() checks if the current pawn position has a matching entry in the pawn hash table. If so, the score from the pawn hash table is used, instead of calculating a score. This saves time.

Other Functions

LoadDiagram

fen is the fen string representing a position.

```
function LoadDiagram(fen) {
 var x, y, n = 0;
 for (x = 0; x < 64; x++) {
  board[x] = EMPTY;
  color[x] = EMPTY;
 }
 for (x = 0; x < 2; x++) {
  for (y = 0; y < 6; y++) {
   bit_pieces[x][y] = 0;
  }
 }
 SetCastle(0);
 currentkey = 0;
 currentlock = 0;
 currentpawnkey = 0;
 currentpawnlock = 0;
 var count = 0, i = 0, j;
 var a;
 for (x = 0; x < fen.length; x++) {
  a = fen.charAt(x);
  if (Number(a) >= 0 && Number(a) <= 8) {
   i += Number(a);
  }
  j = FLIP_BOARD[i];
  if (i < 64) {
    switch (a) {
     case 'K': AddPiece(0, 5, j); Kingloc[0] = j; i++;
break;
     case 'Q': AddPiece(0, 4, j); i++; break;
     case 'R': AddPiece(0, 3, j); i++; break;
     case 'B': AddPiece(0, 2, j); i++; break;
     case 'N': AddPiece(0, 1, j); i++; break;
     case 'P': AddPiece(0, 0, j); i++; break;
     case 'k': AddPiece(1, 5, j); Kingloc[1] = j; i++;
break;
     case 'q': AddPiece(1, 4, j); i++; break;
     case 'r': AddPiece(1, 3, j); i++; break;
     case 'b': AddPiece(1, 2, j); i++; break;
```

```
    case 'n': AddPiece(1, 1, j); i++; break;
    case 'p': AddPiece(1, 0, j); i++; break;
  }
} else {
  if (fen.charAt(x + 1) == 'w') {
    side = 0; xside = 1;
  }
  if (fen.charAt(x + 1) == 'b') {
    side = 1; xside = 0;
  }
  switch (a) {
    case 'K': game_list[0].castle_k0 = 1; break;
    case 'Q': game_list[0].castle_q0 = 1; break;
    case 'k': game_list[0].castle_k1 = 1; break;
    case 'q': game_list[0].castle_q1 = 1; break;
    default: break;
  }
 }
}
}
```

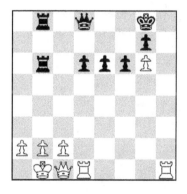

LoadDiagram() parses a fen string and stores the resulting position. It also determines the side to move and the four castling permissions.

- Can white castle kingside?
- Can white castle queenside?
- Can black castle kingside?
- Can black castle queenside?

SaveDiagram

```
function SaveDiagram() {
 var n = 0;
 var a = "";
 var piece = "";
 var j;
 for (var i = 0; i < 64; i++) {
  j = FLIP_BOARD[i];
  if (board[j] != EMPTY && n > 0)
   a += n;
  switch (board[j]) {
   case P: piece = "p"; n = 0; break;
   case N: piece = "n"; n = 0; break;
   case B: piece = "b"; n = 0; break;
   case R: piece = "r"; n = 0; break;
   case Q: piece = "q"; n = 0; break;
   case K: piece = "k"; n = 0; break;
   case EMPTY: n++; break;
   default: break;
  }
  if (color[j] == 0)
   piece = piece.toUpperCase();
  if (color[j] != EMPTY)
   a += piece;
  if (COL[j] == 7) {
   if (n > 0)
    a += n;
   if (j < H8)
    a += "/";
   n = 0;
  }
 }
 if (side == 0)
  a += " w "
 else
  a += " b "
 if (game_list[0].castle_k0 == 1) a += 'K';
 if (game_list[0].castle_q0 == 1) a += 'Q';
 if (game_list[1].castle_k0 == 1) a += 'k';
 if (game_list[1].castle_q0 == 1) a += 'q';
 a += " - 0 1 ";
 return a;
}
```

SaveDiagram() parses a fen string and stores the resulting position. It also determines the side to move and the four castling permissions.

- Can white castle kingside?
- Can white castle queenside?
- Can black castle kingside?
- Can black castle queenside?

IsLegal2

from is the from square of a move. **to** is the to square of a move.

```
function IsLegal2(from, to) {
 first_move[0] = 0;
 ply = 0;
 Gen();
 for (var i = 0; i < first_move[1]; i++) {
  if (move_list[i].from == from && move_list[i].to ==
to) {
   return i;
  }
 }
 /*
 Gen();
 for (var i = first_move[hply]; i <
first_move[hply+1]; i++) {
  if (move_list[i].from == from && move_list[i].to ==
to) {
   return i;
  }
 }
 */
 postMessage("alert=illegal");
 return -1;
}
```

IsLegal2() is a work in progress.

GetResult

```
function GetResult() {
 var count = 0;
 first_move[0] = 0;
```

```
ply = 0;
Gen();
for (var i = 0; i < first_move[1]; i++) {
 if (MakeMove(move_list[i].from, move_list[i].to)) {
  TakeBack();
  count = 1;
  break;
 }
}
if (count == 0) {
 if (Attack(xside, Kingloc[side])) {
  if (side == 0) {
   postMessage("alert=0-1 {Black mates}");
  } else {
   postMessage("alert=1-0 {White mates}");
  }
 } else {
  postMessage("alert=1/2-1/2 {Stalemate}");
 }
 return 1;
}
SetMaterial();
if (Pawn_mat[0] == 0 && Pawn_mat[1] == 0 &&
Piece_mat[0] <= 300 && Piece_mat[1] <= 300) {
 postMessage("alert=1/2-1/2 {Draw by no mating
material}");
 return 1;
}
if (Reps() >= 3) {
 postMessage("alert=1/2-1/2 {Draw by repetition}");
 return 1;
}
if (fifty >= 100) {
 postMessage("alert=1/2-1/2 {Draw by fifty move
rule}");
 fifty = 0;
 return 1;
}
 return 0;
}
```

GetResult() checks the position after a move has been played to see if the player to move has any legal moves. If not then the game has ended and it is either checkmate or stalemate. It also checks for draws by no mating material by either side, a draw by repetition or a draw by the 50 move rule. It makes no difference if a human or engine has moved.

Both sides have no pawns and no more than a bishop (worth 300) so *alert=1/2-1/2 {Draw by no mating material}* is posted, and the game is drawn.

SetMaterial

```
function SetMaterial() {
 for (var s = 0; s < 2; s++) {
  Pawn_mat[s] = 0;
  Piece_mat[s] = 0;
 }
 for (var x = 0; x < 64; x++) {
  if (board[x] < K) {
   if (board[x] == P) {
    Pawn_mat[color[x]] += 100;
   } else {
    Piece_mat[color[x]] += piece_value[board[x]];
   }
  }
 }
}
```

SetMaterial() calculates the pawn material score and piece material score for both sides. This is used by **GetResult()**.

Debug

n is a string that is displayed in an alert box.

```
function Debug(n) {
```

```
try {
  throw "error";
}
catch (err) {
  postMessage("alert=" + n);
}
}
```

Debug() may be called while debugging. The try-catch block throws an error which causes an alert box to pop up. This will display the string **n**. Here is an example of how it could be used. **AddKey()** a good place to catch errors.

```
function AddKey(s, p, x) {
try {
currentkey ^= piecehash[s][p][x];
currentlock ^= piecelock[s][p][x];
}
catch (err) {
var a1 = "alert= " + err + " addkey s " + s + " p "
+ p + " x " + x;
postMessage(a1 + " ply " + ply + " hply " + hply);
}
}
```

ShowList

```
function ShowList() {
 var s = "";
 var x;
 for (x = first_move[ply]; x < first_move[ply + 1]; x+
+) {
  s += Algebraic(move_list[x].from) + "-" +
Algebraic(move_list[x].to);
  s += " " + move_list[x].score + "\n";
 }
 s += " num " + (first_move[ply + 1] -
first_move[ply]);
 postMessage("alert= " + s);
}
```

ShowList() displays a list of legal moves. It may be called from **Debug()**, while debugging.

Displaying the Chess Position

There are several ways of displaying a Chess position on a web page. One way is to use Chess fonts, though it requires installing the Chess fonts.

Another approach is to use a canvas on which the board and pieces can be drawn.

I have chosen the simplest and most direct approach which is to create an 8x8 table in HTML. It will be helpful to understand how tables work in HTML. A table starts with a <table> tag and ends with a </table>; tag.

Each cell in the table represents a square on the chessboard. This makes it easy to detect which square is clicked on and also to draw the Chess pieces and empty squares.

```
<table align="center" id="tblMain" border="0"
style="cursor: pointer;" cellspacing=0 cellpadding=0>
<tr><td></td><td></td><td></td><td></td><td></
td><td></td><td></td><td></td></tr>
<tr><td></td><td></td><td></td><td></td><td></
td><td></td><td></td><td></td></tr>
<tr><td></td><td></td><td></td><td></td><td></
td><td></td><td></td><td></td></tr>
<tr><td></td><td></td><td></td><td></td><td></
```

```
td><td></td><td></td><td></td></tr>
<tr><td></td><td></td><td></td><td></td><td></
td><td></td><td></td><td></td></tr>
<tr><td></td><td></td><td></td><td></td><td></
td><td></td><td></td><td></td></tr>
<tr><td></td><td></td><td></td><td></td><td></
td><td></td><td></td><td></td></tr>
<tr><td></td><td></td><td></td><td></td><td></
td><td></td><td></td><td></td></tr>
</table>
```

The style attribute causes the mouse pointer to change when it moves over the chessboard. Each pair of td tags represents a cell in the table. This is the HTML code for the chessboard without code within each of the 64 td tags containing any code. It is easy to see that there are 8 rows of 8 pairs of td tags.

Each cell contains an **img** tag. Both **td** tags and **img** tags have an **id**. The td id helps to determine which cell the user has clicked on. The IMG id allows the image to be changed dynamically with JavaScript.

The squares have an id of 0-63 inclusive. Ids need to be unique so an arbitrary 100 is added to the id of a cell.

```
<tr><td id=156><img id=56></td>
```

For example, the A8 square which is the top left corner has this html code. There is similar code for all the cells.

GetBoard

a is a string representing the board.

```
function GetBoard(a) {
  for (var x = 0; x < 64; x++)
   web_board[x] = Number(a.charAt(x));
  for (var x = 64; x < 128; x++)
   web_color[x - 64] = Number(a.charAt(x));
}
  var tbl = document.getElementById("tblMain");
  if (tbl != null) {
```

```
    for (var i = 0; i < tbl.rows.length; i++) {
      for (var j = 0; j < tbl.rows[i].cells.length; j++)
        tbl.rows[i].cells[j].onclick = function ()
{ GetValue(this); };
      }
    }
}
```

GetBoard() is used to determine which cell is clicked on. It first updates **web_board** and **web_color**. It then loops through all the cells in the table representing the board. **onclick** detects if a cell has been clicked on. If so, **GetValue()** is called.

GetValue

cell is a square on the chessboard.

```
function GetValue(cell) {
  var p = cell.id - 100;
  if (flipboard == 1)
    p = 63 - p;
  if (start == -1) {
    if (web_board[p] == EMPTY) {
      DisplayText("no piece on " + Algebraic(p));
      return 0;
    }
    if (web_color[p] == 1 - side) {
      DisplayText(" wrong side " + Algebraic(p));
      return 0;
    }
    if (web_color[p] == side) {
      DisplayText("start square " + Algebraic(p));
      start = p;
      return 0;
    }
  }
  else {
    if (web_color[p] == side) {
      DisplayText("start square " + Algebraic(p));
      start = p;
      return 0;
    }
    dest = p;
    w.postMessage("play=" + start + "=" + dest);
    SetBoard();
```

```
   var piece = web_board[start];
   var capture = web_board[dest];
   DisplayText(LongAlgebraic(piece, start, dest,
capture));
   start = -1;
   if (player[xside] == HUMAN)
     return 0;
   xside = side; side = side ^ 1;
   SetButtons(true);
   Go();
   SetButtons(false);
   const d = new Date();
   var time = d.getTime();
   DisplayText("alert=time 1 " + time);
   SetButtons(false);
   ply = 0;
   first_move[0] = 0;
   SetBoard();
  }
}
```

The number of the cell that is clicked on is **cell.id**. Subtracting the arbitrary 100 from this converts it to a square id.

If the board has been flipped, i.e. Black is on the bottom, then **p=63-p** gets the correct square. If an empty square is clicked on, a message is displayed. If a piece of the wrong side is clicked on, a message is displayed, otherwise, the square becomes the start of a move.

A second click determines the destination square of the move. The sides are switched, the engine makes a move and the game continues.

Images

jpg images are used. There are 24 images representing the pieces and 2 more for empty squares. There are:

- Six images for white pieces on light squares.
- Six images for white pieces on dark squares.
- Six images for black pieces on light squares.
- Six images for black pieces on dark squares.

- An image for an empty light square.
- An image for an empty dark square.

The filenames of these images are stored in the arrays WhiteImg[6]
[2] and BlackImg[6][2]. These arrays are populated by the
LoadImages function which is called once when the web page is
loaded.

SetBoard

```
function SetBoard() {
 var x, y, a2;
 var folder;
 folder = "pieces/";
 for (x = 0; x < 64; x++) {
  if (flipboard == 0)
   y = x;
  else
   y = 63 - x;
  if (web_color[y] == 0)
   a2 = WhiteImg[web_board[y]][SQUARE_COLOR[y]];
  else
   a2 = BlackImg[web_board[y]][SQUARE_COLOR[y]];
  document.getElementById(x).src = folder + a2;
 }
}
```

SetBoard() is used to display the Chess position. It loops through
all 64 squares and assigns an image to each square. **c[y]** is used to
determine the colour of the piece, while **s[y]** is used to determine
the colour of the square. If the board has been *flipped* then 63-x
will flip the square.

Input and Output

A form is used for user input and to display output.

```
<form>
<input type="button" id="new" name="newgame" value="New Game" onclick="NewGame();">
<br>
<label for "fen">Paste fen position
<input type="text" id="fen" name="fen" value="">
<br>
<input type="button" id="load" name="load" value="Load Position" onclick="LoadDiagram();">
<input type="button" id="addlevel" name="addlevel" value="+" onclick="AddLevel();">
<input type="button" id="sublevel" name="sublevel" value="-" onclick="SubLevel();">
<label for "level">Select Level
<table border=1>
<tr>
<td id=level>1</td>
</tr>
</table>
<input type="button" id="white" name="white" value="White" onclick="SetPlayer(0);">
<input type="button" id="black" name="black" value="Black" onclick="SetPlayer(1);">
<table border=1>
<tr>
<td id=players></td>
</tr>
</table>
<input type="button" id="go" name="go" value="Go" onclick="Go();">
<br>
<input type="button" id="flipbb" name="flipb" value="Flip Board" onclick="FlipBoard();">
<br>
<input type="button" id="takeback" name="takeback" value="Take Back" onclick="TakeBackMove();">
<br>
<label for "info">Info
<table border=1 width=250 height=50>
<tr>
<td id=info></td>
</tr>
</table>
</td>
</form>
```

A button triggers a function when it is clicked on.

New Game

NewGame() starts a new game.

Load Position

Loads a position from a .fen file and displays the board.

Level

The + and - buttons allows the user to increase or decrease the playing level. The playing level is the depth the engine searches. The level cannot be less than 1 or greater than 32. The deeper the level, the longer the engine will take.

White and Black

The white and black buttons toggle between a human and computer player for that colour.

Flip Board

Toggles the flipboard flag and displays the board.

Take Back

Takes back the last move, whether it was played by a human or the engine.

board.html

The following code is in board.html.

```
var player = [0,0];
var player_type = ["human","computer"];
```

player[] stores whether a player is human or computer.

```
var WhiteImg =  new Create2DArray(20,6);
var BlackImg =  new Create2DArray(20,6);
```

WhiteImg[] and **BlackImg[]** are arrays of images which are used to display the position.

```
var start, dest;
```

start represents the start square of a move, while **dest** represents the destination square of a move.

```
var root_from = 0,root_to = 0,root_score = 0;
```

root_from and **root_to** represent the move chosen by the engine. **root_score** represents it's score.

```
var flipboard=0;
```

If **flipboard** is 0 then white is at the bottom, else black is at the bottom.

```
var E1=4;
var E8=60;
```

The E1 and E8 squares are used with castling.

```
var max_nodes=0;
```

max_nodes represents the maximum number of positions the engine can search.

```
var max_depth;
```

max_depth represents the maximum depth the engine can search.

```
var Safari=1;
```

The Safari browser can run a web worker offline.

```
start = -1;
```

start is initialised to -1.

```
var side = 0;
```

side is 0 or 1 (white or black).

```
var first, second, line;
```

first, second and **line** are used with messages.

```
DisplayPlayers();
SetImages();
if(Safari==1)
{
  startWorker();
}
function startWorker()
{
  if (typeof(Worker) !== "undefined")
  {
  if (typeof(w) == "undefined")
   w = new Worker("engine2.JavaScript");
  w.onmessage = function(event)
  {
   line=event.data;
   first=FirstPart(line);
   second=SecondPart(line);
   if(first=="add")
   {
   DisplayText(second);
   }
```

```
if(first=="alert")
{
alert(second);
}
if(first=="cb")
{
GetBoard(second);
SetBoard();
}
if(first=="side")
{
side=(second);
xside=side^1;
}
if(first=="info")
DisplayInfo(second);
}
}
else
alert("Sorry! No Web Worker support.");
}
```

startWorker() creates a worker. The **onmessage** function responds to messages from the worker to board.html. The message is a string that is divided into two parts by the FirstPart() and SecondPart() functions. The parts are separated by an equals sign. A different function is called depending on the first part.

```
function stopWorker()
{
  w.terminate();
  w = undefined;
}
```

stopWorker() is used to terminate the worker.

```
w.postMessage("set");
function SetPlayer(s)
{
player[s] = player[s]^1;
DisplayPlayers();
}
```

SetPlayer() toggles the given player between 0 and 1, i.e. human or computer.

```
function DisplayPlayers()
{
var a="White "+player_type[player[0]]+" Black
"+player_type[player[1]];
var x1=document.getElementById('players');
x1.innerHTML = a;
}
```

DisplayPlayers() shows whether players are human or computer.

```
function FlipBoard()
{
flipboard=flipboard^1;
SetBoard();
}
```

FlipBoard() flips the board and redraws it. The operation ^1 causes **flipboard** to change to 1 if it is 0 and vice versa.

```
function NewGame()
{
w.postMessage("new");
}
```

NewGame() posts a message which sets a new game up.

```
function Go()
{
if(player[side]==1)
{
w.postMessage("depth="+max_depth);
w.postMessage("think="+side);
w.postMessage("info");
DisplayInfo();
SetBoard();
}
}
```

Go() passes max_depth and side to the worker, starts think() and displays information about the move.

```
function DisplayText(a)
{
var x1=document.getElementById('box');
x1.innerHTML = a;
}
```

DisplayText() displays text in a textbox.

```
function DisplayInfo(a)
{
var x1=document.getElementById('info');
x1.innerHTML = a;
}
```

DisplayInfo() displays information about the move.

```
function TakeBackMove()
{
w.postMessage("takeback");
}
```

TakeBackMove() posts a message which causes a move to be taken back.

```
function GetSquareNumber(sq)
{
var file, rank, square;
file =  sq.substring(0, 1);
rank =  sq.substring(1, 2);
square = file.charCodeAt(0) - 96 + (rank - 1) * 8;
return square;
}
```

GetSquareNumber() returns the number of the given square. For example, **a1** returns 0. The numbers are in the range 0-63.

```
function AddLevel()
{
if(max_depth<32)
  max_depth++;
var x1=document.getElementById('level');
x1.innerHTML = max_depth;
}
```

AddLevel() increases the playing level, which is stored in **max_depth**. The level cannot be greater than 32. This makes the engine play stronger, but also slower.

```
function SubLevel()
{
if(max_depth>1)
  max_depth--;
var x1=document.getElementById('level');
x1.innerHTML = max_depth;
}
```

SubLevel() reduces the playing level, which is stored in **max_depth**. The level cannot be less than 1.

```
function LoadDiagram()
{
var a = document.getElementById("fen").value;
w.postMessage("diag="+a);
}
```

Messages

onmessage

```
onmessage = function (event) {
 var line = event.data;
 var a = "", a2 = "";
 a = FirstPart(line);
 a2 = SecondPart(line);
 var move, from, to;
 var a1;
 switch (a) {
  case "set":
   SetUp();
   postMessage("add=engine loaded");
   break;
  case "new":
   InitBoard();
   CopyBoard();
   postMessage("add=");
   break;
  case "cas1":
   SetCastle(1);
   break;
  case "depth":
   max_depth = Number(a2);
   break;
  case "time":
   max_time = Number(a2);
   break;
  case "takeback":
   if (hply > 0) {
    TakeBack();
    CopyBoard();
    postMessage("add=");
   }
   break;
  case "forward":
   ForwardMove();
   CopyBoard();
   postMessage("add=");
   break;
  case "think":
   CompMove(a2);
```

```
    GetResult();
    break;
  case "diag":
   LoadDiagram(a2);
   CopyBoard();
   postMessage("add=");
   break;
  case "save"://
   postMessage("fen=" + SaveDiagram());
   break;
  case "board"://
   CopyBoard();
   break;
  case "play":
   move = a2;
   from = FirstPart(a2);
   to = SecondPart(a2);
   if (IsLegal2(from, to) == -1) {
    postMessage("illegal=" + from + " " + to);
    return;
   }
   MakeMove(from, to);
   CopyBoard();
   break;
 }
}
```

The **onmessage** function responds to messages from the worker to board.html. The message is a string that is divided into two parts by the FirstPart() and SecondPart() functions. The parts are separated by an equals sign. A different function is called depending on the text in the first part.

```
function ForwardMove() {
 //Debug("alert=for 1 " +
Algebraic(game_list[hply].from) +
Algebraic(game_list[hply].to));
 MakeMove(game_list[hply].from, game_list[hply].to);
 CopyBoard();
}
```

CompMove

```
function CompMove(a2) {
 const start = Date.now();
```

```
Think();
const millis = Date.now() - start;
var nps = 0;
if (millis > 0) nps = nodes * 1000 / millis;
side = Number(a2);
xside = side ^ 1;
var piece = board[root_from];
var capture = board[root_to];
MakeMove(root_from, root_to);
CopyBoard();
var a1 = LongAlgebraic(piece, root_from, root_to,
capture) + " depth " + max_depth + "
 score " + root_score + "
";
 a1 += " Time " + millis + " Nodes " + nodes + " Nodes
per second " + Math.round(nps);
 postMessage("info=" + a1);
}
```

CompMove()

- Calls Think() to make the engine choose a move.
- Calculates the time taken.
- Makes the engine move.
- Copies the board to the web page.
- Displays the move, depth, score and time etc.

FirstPart

```
function FirstPart(a) {
 var a2 = "";
 if (a == undefined) return a2;
 for (var x = 0; x < a.length; x++) {
  if (a.charAt(x) == "=") break;
  a2 += a.charAt(x);
 }
 return a2;
}
```

FirstPart() extracts the part of a string before an =.

SecondPart

```
function SecondPart(a) {
```

```
var a2 = "";
if (a == undefined) return a2;
var flag = 0;
for (var x = 0; x < a.length; x++) {
 if (flag == 1) a2 += a.charAt(x);
 if (a.charAt(x) == "=") flag = 1;
}
return a2;
}
```

SecondPart() extracts the part of a string after an =. **FirstPart()** and **SecondPart()** allow a string to be divided into two parts. They are used to read messages sent with **postMessage()**. **FirstPart** and **SecondPart** are used to help parse a string containing an = sign. The string was sent by **PostMessage**. This allows more complex instructions to be sent with **postMessage()**.

CopyBoard

```
function CopyBoard() {
 var a = "";
 for (var x = 0; x < 64; x++) {
  a += board[x];
 }
 for (var x = 0; x < 64; x++) {
  a += color[x];
 }
 postMessage("cb=" + a);
 postMessage("side=" + side);
}
```

CopyBoard() copies the board to a string and sends it from the worker to the html page.

PostBoard

```
function PostBoard() {
 var s = "";
 var k = "";
 for (var x = 0; x < 64; x++) {
  if (color[x] == 0) k = "w";
  if (color[x] == 1) k = "b";
  switch (board[x]) {
   case "p":
```

```
    s += (k + "p" + Algebraic(x) + " ");
    break;
  case "n":
    s += (k + "n" + Algebraic(x) + " ");
    break;
  case "b":
    s += (k + "b" + Algebraic(x) + " ");
    break;
  case "r":
    s += (k + "r" + Algebraic(x) + " ");
    break;
  case "q":
    s += (k + "q" + Algebraic(x) + " ");
    break;
  case "k":
    s += (k + "k" + Algebraic(x) + " ");
    break;
  default:
    break;
  }
 }
 postMessage("pb=" + s);
}
```

PostBoard() copies the board to a string and sends it from the worker to the html page.

Optimizing the Code

JavaScript is an interpreted language which means that white space, such as blank spaces, blank lines etc. slows down loading time. For this reason, there is less use of white space to ident code as with a compiled language.

It is possible to **minify** JavaScript code by using a utility that removes the white space from the code. Unfortunately, this makes the code almost unreadable and impossible to edit easily. I have experimented with minifying the code and it does make it execute faster. I suggest googling minify JavaScript to find a utility for minifying the code.

FireFox and JavaScript

The Firefox browser allows you to use a compiled version of JavaScript which runs very fast. There is a very strong version of the *StockFish* program which does this. However, it was very slow to load and took several minutes on my system.

Possible Improvements

The ways to make a Chess engine stronger include:

- Make it run faster.
- Improve the search algorithm.
- Improve the evaluation.
- Adding an opening library.
- Add endgame knowledge.

Speed

The speed is increased by the use of look-up tables instead of calculating. More look-up tables may be possible.

Test positions may be used to see if changes in code lead to a speed increase or not.

Search

A specialised move generation function for check evasion would greatly reduce the number of positions that need to be searched when a player is in check.

More frontier pruning could reduce the number of positions that are not worth looking at low depths.

Reductions are little used. More reductions could increase the depth of search, but that have to be used carefully.

Evaluation

The evaluation is very basic. Most evaluation is material plus the square a piece or pawn is on.

There are a myriad ways how the square score tables can be altered to change the engine's style. This is one way to experiment with the evaluation.

The only type of weak pawn evaluated is an isolated pawn. Doubled pawns which are not isolated, are not weak in themselves. They may result in an ineffective pawn majority, but this is more complex to code.

Apart from getting a bonus for having a pawn in front of the king, the engine does not recognise a pawn shield. More complex evaluation could give a bonus for pawns on other squares.

Rooks get a bonus for the 1st, 7th and 8th ranks but the engine doesn't recognise open or half-open files. The engine doesn't recognise when a bishop is blocked by pawns. Evaluation might be better if the number of squares line pieces could move to is counted, but would slow down the evaluation. Evaluation can be a trade-off between speed and quality.

The engine has a tendency to rush the king towards the centre when the opponent has no queen. A more subtle approach may give better results.

Opening

An opening library would allow to instantly play moves that are in it's *opening book*. It is beneficial for the engine to be able to detect transpositions. One approach is to prefill the hash table with opening positions with the next move to be played.

An opening library would also allow to vary its openings considerably. It can be dull if it plays the same openings each time. The engine varies its openings somewhat by default, if several games are played without restarting. This was accidental, I suspect it is because the hash tables are not being cleared between games.

Endgame

The engine's endgame knowledge is minimal. It knows that a lone minor piece is not enough to mate. It has no trouble mating with a rook or queen against a lone king. It understands passed pawns need to be pushed. However, it does not see deeply enough in long endgame variations.

It would benefit by knowledge of the *square of the pawn*, especially in pawn endgames. The square of the pawn would allow it to see up to 10 ply deeper, at very little cost. For example, if white had a pawn on a3 and black had a king on h3, it could be used to see if the king could catch the passed pawn or not.

Endgame tablebases allow an engine to instantly look up the strongest move in certain endgames with only a few pieces on each side.

Feel free to experiment with the code.

About the Author

Bill Jordan was taught Chess on his 7th birthday by his father using a Chess set carved by his grandfather. Four years later he started reading Chess books. Four years later he became Victorian Junior Chess champion.

He later became Australian junior Chess champion, Victorian Chess champion, Australian correspondence Chess champion, South Australian Chess champion and Australian senior champion. Since the age of 17, Bill Jordan has represented Australia in international Chess events in Malaysia, Yugoslavia, Mexico and China.

Since 1981 Bill has been a life member and has been president of the Melbourne Chess club, one of the oldest Chess clubs in the world.

He is an enthusiastic Chess software programmer who has taught and written manuals for Chess as well as IT and lateral thinking. He has also written numerous articles for Chess magazines. Bill is an experienced individual and group coach, who has a wide and deep understanding of Chess.